The
Incomparable
Valley

"And this our life, exempt from public haunt,
Finds tongues in trees, books in the running brooks,
Sermons in stones, and good in everything."
                              Shakespeare, *As You Like It*

The

Incomparable

Valley

a geologic interpretation
of the Yosemite

by François E. Matthes

edited by Fritiof Fryxell

University of California Press · Berkeley, Los Angeles, London

To all who love the mountains,

particularly those who come to see,

and seeing, wonder and wish to understand

University of California Press, Berkeley and Los Angeles, California

University of California Press, Ltd., London, England

SBN: 520-00827-8

Printed in the United States of America
Designed by John B. Goetz

890

Foreword

The fates decreed that François Matthes should not write his long-planned "Yosemite Book." Yet his friends and admirers everywhere will feel that the present volume is, indeed, his work. Fritiof Fryxell, for many years a co-worker and intimate friend of Dr. Matthes, has guaranteed that this shall be so.

No one among the many colleagues identified with the Matthes school of geological research in the Sierra Nevada could be more self-effacing and more successful in blending the editor's contribution with the author's original interpretation. Dr. Fryxell, a geologist, teacher, and author, is possessed also of a fine appreciation of the humanities. He has specialized in research and interpretive programs of the National Park Service for more than twenty years—a work which prepared him very well to address the Matthes material to the host of lovers of the Yosemite scene.

In the pages which follow there is little identification of the personal philosophy of Dr. Fryxell. It is reflected in some degree in the following quotation, which has been taken from a recent address he delivered in Davenport, Iowa:

An old legend tells of a saintly man who died and went to Judgment. Being a saint he was also humble, and not sure of his reception. To the Almighty, therefore, he recited with breathless haste all the deeds he could think of that were good. These were many, and he did not pause till of necessity, when out of breath. Taking this chance the Almighty asked him, wistfully, "But what did you think of my beautiful world?" Alas, the man had had no time to look at that.

Many another besides this good man has lived oblivious to the beautiful world. But there are those, and many of them too, who are so keenly sensitive to the beauty round about them that if deprived of it they cannot be truly happy, for from it stem their deepest satisfactions and enduring inspiration. To such it is a matter of no small concern that the heritage of beauty which is ours in rocks and rills, in woods and templed hills, shall not be squandered, but cherished as a precious legacy.

Dr. Matthes, also, was imbued with the idea of cherishing natural beauty. Readers everywhere will be grateful to Dr. Fryxell and to Mrs. Matthes for fulfilling François Matthes' intention of making this store of scientific knowledge and human appreciation of the drama in earth forces available in popular form. The subject and its nontechnical style will appeal strongly to those concerned with any aspect of the interpretation of the Sierra Nevada, and in the historical view it rounds out most beautifully the inspiring story of a great scientist's devotion to his studies and to his fellow man.

CARL P. RUSSELL
Superintendent,
Yosemite National Park

Preface

Perhaps the reader will share the editor's feeling that the writing of books, like some other estates, should not be entered into lightly. If this be so under ordinary circumstances, how much more is it not true when one writes on behalf of another? Throughout his work on this book, the editor has sought never to forget that this must be, so far as possible, the book which François Matthes was to have written but never did.

The editor would not have had the temerity to accept a responsibility so great but for some previous acquaintance with the problems involved. This acquaintance was gained, in the first place, on a memorable excursion into Yosemite Valley and the High Sierra with François Matthes in the summer of 1936; subsequently in his association with Dr. Matthes in developing an exhibit plan for the geology displays of the museum at Yosemite National Park, a project of the National Park Service; and, finally, through the years of friendly association which followed. During the years 1942 to 1946 the contacts were particularly close, as Dr. Matthes and the editor were then co-workers in the United States Geological Survey, at Washington, D.C. As war work made necessary his continuance with the Survey beyond the age of retirement, and so the postponement of cherished personal projects, Dr. Matthes more than once told of his plans for a "Yosemite book" to be written after the war.

When he did retire, in 1947, after fifty-one years of distinguished service to the government, he and his wife Edith drove from Washington to California; and here, in their promised land, they established a little home in El Cerrito, on the Berkeley Hills overlooking San Francisco Bay and facing the Golden Gate. Now at last he would find peace and time to write. He would allow himself first the joy of writing the Yosemite book; then the unfinished government reports on the Sierra Nevada, together with shorter papers, would be completed in orderly succession. But before he had set his hand to the writing, in the early morning hours of April 18, 1948, he suffered a heart attack. On June 21 his brave spirit left the spent body, and his work was done.

But friends continued to hope that the Yosemite book might still be written. The basic scientific studies, the fruits of decades of research on the Sierra Nevada by François Matthes, were published and available. There were, further, voluminous private notes of miscellaneous character, as well as unpublished lectures—sources which Dr. Matthes would, in all probability, have utilized in his writing. Might it not be possible, from these, to prepare a book which would in a measure realize his hopes and meet the insistent demand for its publication? It was the writer's privilege to ascertain, on behalf of the University of California Press, what could be done.

So, in the summer of 1949, this book took shape. It was, so to speak, woven together. The strands of which it was made were indeed of various materials, and derived from many sources; but each was selected and used with care, in order that the desired final product might result—a comprehensive and unified account setting forth François Matthes' interpretations of the Yosemite and the Sierra Nevada, expressed, so far as possible, in his own language.

The use of Matthes' actual words was not, of course, always possible; and where essential elements were lacking the editor had to supply them—introductory, connecting, and concluding sentences and paragraphs, as well as many sections of text to bridge longer gaps: new strands, these which it is to be hoped may harmonize with the others, blending into the general fabric so as to be indistinguishable from it.

Naturally, the principal published works of François Matthes have been important sources for the volume: his *Geologic History of the Yo-*

semite Valley (Professional Paper 160, U. S. Geological Survey); the chapter he contributed to *The Sierra Nevada: The Range of Light;* the text he wrote for the topographic map of the Yosemite Valley; and other papers. True, some sections borrowed from these sources had to be condensed; but others, as for example those that comprise most of chapters 8 and 9, could be used with only such minor changes as fitted them into their new context, and many reappear without change.

Whatever François Matthes published had much the same exquisite finish that characterized the marvelous draftsmanship of his topographic maps. For although he was born and reared in Europe, where he was educated successively in the Dutch, French, and German languages before he began to learn English, he attained a lucidity and beauty of expression in our language unsurpassed among contemporary American geologists. Thus the extraordinary situation of an editor being able to extract, verbatim, passages from technical articles for inclusion in a volume designed for nontechnical readers.

Selections from unpublished notes were not so easy to make. The perfection of the published papers quite belied the effort which had gone into them. Surely, few scientific writers have been so concerned with effectiveness of expression and worked so assiduously to achieve it! With François Matthes each thought was an entity which could be expressed in many ways, and discovery of the most effective way was a problem to the solution of which he spared neither time nor effort. He would rewrite a paragraph or page over and over again, experimenting with the order, phrasing, and emphasis. The resultant versions that had merit, and were potentially usable in different situations, were filed away for future reference. To choose from many alternative renderings of the same ideas has been difficult but rewarding, for they have yielded many a usable strand. So, from the unpublished materials as well as the published ones, selected phrases were woven into sentences, sentences into paragraphs, and paragraphs into chapters. Most important of the unpublished sources were the manuscripts of the three LeConte Memorial Lectures, which François Matthes delivered at Yosemite National Park on July 8–10, 1919, as part of a series sponsored by the University of California Extension Division, in memory of the noted professor, Joseph LeConte.

Many readers, after an introduction to the origin of Yosemite Valley, will wish to pursue this fascinating subject further. They should, then, turn to François Matthes' great treatise on the subject, *Geologic History of the Yosemite Valley,* one of the classics of geological literature and a well-nigh inexhaustible source of information on the subject. They should not neglect to consult, also, its Appendix, contributed by Frank

C. Calkins, which describes the granitic rocks of the Yosemite region.

In the preparation of this book, Edith Matthes has been the editor's close and devoted associate. Without her understanding of François Matthes' desires for the book and her knowledge of the private sources it manifestly could not have been written. The fine literary sense and intimate, firsthand acquaintance with the Sierra Nevada which she shared with her husband enabled her to offer many suggestions incorporated in these pages. This invaluable assistance, the extent of which can hardly be overstated, the editor gratefully acknowledges.

Acknowledgment is also made to Mr. David R. Brower and Mr. August Frugé, of the University of California Press, whose deep personal interest was directly responsible for preparation of this book, and whose thoughtful planning for it is reflected in its format; to Mr. Ansel Adams, without whose incomparable photographs any attempt to interpret "The Incomparable Valley" would indeed be incomplete; to Dr. Howel Williams of the Department of Geology, University of California, for a critical review of the manuscript of this book, and constructive suggestions which have been incorporated in it; and, finally, to the Vanguard Press for permission to quote extensively from François Matthes' chapter in *The Sierra Nevada, The Range of Light*.

It is evident that this book does not purport to present much that is new. Nor does it attempt to trace the steps by which our present understanding of the Yosemite and the Sierra Nevada has been reached, or assign credit to the many individuals who have contributed to that understanding. This has already been done by Dr. Matthes, fully and fairly, in Professional Paper 160 and elsewhere.

The book has, rather, been written solely with a view to serving the purpose which François Matthes always had in mind for it: to interpret the Yosemite and the Sierra Nevada to all who love the mountains, particularly those who come to see, and seeing, wonder and wish to understand.

FRITIOF FRYXELL

Contents

Bird's-Eye View of Yosemite Valley
and the High Sierra

RF	Ribbon Fall	MW	Mount Watkins	LC	Liberty Cap
EC	El Capitan	E	Echo Peaks	B	Mount Broderick
EP	Eagle Peak	C	Clouds Rest	SD	Sentinel Dome
YF	Top of Yosemite Falls	SM	Sunrise Mountain	G	Glacier Point
GC	Government Center	Q	Quarter Domes	SR	Sentinel Rock
IC	Indian Creek	HD	Half Dome	T	Taft Point
R	Royal Arches	M	Mount Maclure	CS	Cathedral Spires
W	Washington Column	L	Mount Lyell	CR	Cathedral Rocks
TC	Tenaya Canyon	F	Mount Florence	BV	Bridalveil Fall
ML	Mirror Lake	BP	Bunnell Point	LT	Leaning Tower
ND	North Dome	CC	Cascade Cliffs	DP	Dewey Point
BD	Basket Dome	LY	Little Yosemite	MR	Merced River

Physiographic Setting of the Sierra Nevada (reproduced from Map of the Landforms of the United States, courtesy of Professor Erwin Raisz, Harvard University, and Ginn and Company).

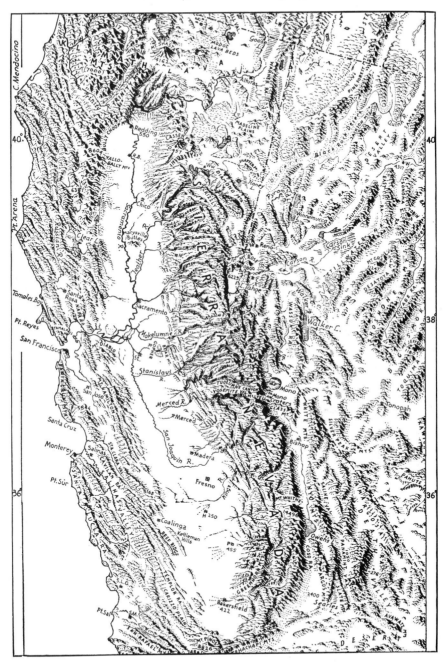

Plate 1. The climax of the east front of the Sierra Nevada, in the Mount Whitney region, here an escarpment rising nearly two miles above Owens Valley. Lone Pine Peak dominates at the left; Mount Whitney is the high peak in the right background; the Alabama Hills and the floor of Owens Valley are in the foreground.

The view shows the narrow and abrupt character of the east slope of the tilted earth block which gives rise to the Sierra Nevada. This slope follows a great line of fracturing and displacement: the Sierra fault. In striking contrast, the opposite slope of the Sierra Nevada—the inclined top of the block, in which Yosemite Valley and the other great canyons of the range are carved—is exceedingly broad and slopes very gently toward the west. Photograph by Ansel Adams.

Plate 2. Yosemite Valley in the broad-valley stage (end of Miocene epoch). The Yosemite region, after ages of stream erosion following the first Sierra uplift, was reduced to a land of rolling hills. The valley was broad and less than 1,000 feet deep. The Merced River wound sluggishly from side to side, and tributary streams joined it without waterfalls. Hardwood forests flourished in a mild, rainy climate.

Plate 3. The mountain-valley stage (end of Pliocene epoch). The second Sierra uplift had accelerated the Merced River; as a result, the Yosemite was cut 800 feet deeper. It lay between hilly uplands, and from hanging valleys on those uplands the lesser side streams cascaded. The climate had become cooler and drier, and the forests consisted mainly of conifers, including sequoias.

Plate 4. The canyon stage (early in Pleistocene epoch). The third and greatest uplift had raised the Sierra Nevada almost to its present height. The Merced, now a swift mountain torrent, had deepened the Yosemite to a 3,000-foot canyon. All the side streams except Tenaya Creek cascaded boisterously from hanging valleys. The winters were becoming more severe and the forests sparser. The Ice Age was coming on.

Plate 5. The second (El Portal) glacial stage. The Yosemite Glacier filled the valley nearly to the brink and reached down to the vicinity of El Portal. All the northern upland, except the tops of El Capitan and Eagle Peak, was mantled with ice. The southern upland bore only one small glacier, in Bridalveil Basin. Half Dome rose 700 feet above the ice flood. The Cathedral Rocks were submerged.

Plate 6. The third and latest (Wisconsin) glacial stage. The Yosemite Glacier of this stage was relatively small, and reached little beyond Bridalveil Fall. The valley had been excavated to its present depth and width. Its sloping sides were transformed to cliffs, and the cascades to leaping waterfalls. Hardy vegetation held its own in the valley below the glacier and even on the uplands above the rim.

Plate 7. After the Ice Age and before the filling of Lake Yosemite. When the glacier finally withdrew from the valley, there remained a beautiful lake, impounded by a terminal moraine. The Merced River brought down vast quantities of gravel and sand, and built a delta in the lake. In the course of time, ancient Lake Yosemite was filled, and replaced by the present level valley floor.

Plates 2–7, from paintings at the Yosemite National Park Museum, were made under the scientific supervision of François Matthes, by Herbert A. Collins, Sr., and Herbert A. Collins, Jr.

Plate 8. Mount Lyell and the Lyell Glacier in the center background; the Lyell Fork of the Tuolumne River in the foreground. In the Ice Age, Mount Lyell was a center from which great glaciers descended into the Tuolumne Canyon, Yosemite Valley, and other canyons of the Sierra Nevada. Photograph by Ansel Adams.

Plate 9. The Dana Glacier lies on the north face of Mount Dana in a shaded cirque excavated by a much larger glacier of the Ice Age. At its front are several moraine ridges composed of rock debris. Photograph by G. K. Gilbert.

Plate 10. View eastward from Mount Hoffmann, with Mount Conness to the left and Mount Dana to the right; Tuolumne Meadows in the middle distance. Part of the ice field which once occupied this basin overflowed the Tuolumne-Merced Divide to the right (southeast) of Mount Hoffmann and continued down Tenaya Canyon to Yosemite Valley. Photograph by Ansel Adams.

Plate 11. At the right, the face of Matthes Crest, which formerly rose as an island (**nunatak**) from the ice field that overswept the Tuolumne-Merced Divide. The Clark Range is in the background. Photograph by Ansel Adams.

Plate 12. Telephoto of Mount Conness from Tenaya Lake, looking northeast. Part of the Tuolumne ice field descended through this canyon into Yosemite Valley. Photograph by Ansel Adams.

Plate 13. The great facade of Clouds Rest, from Mount Watkins. Composed of massive granite, exfoliating at the surface, the façade is 4,700 feet high. The highest level reached by the Tenaya Glacier can be determined approximately from the sculpture of the spurs. Photograph by François Matthes.

Plate 14. The Giant Stairway, from Glacier Point. In the center is Nevada Fall, which leaps from the upper step, flanked on the left by Liberty Cap. Below is Vernal Fall, which leaps from the lower step. On the far side of the Little Yosemite, which is behind Liberty Cap, are the water-streaked Cascade Cliffs. Beyond are the snow-mantled peaks of the High Sierra. At the left is Mount Florence. Photograph by Ansel Adams.

Plate 15. Back view of Liberty Cap and Mount Broderick. Their curving backs (stoss sides) and crowns were ground and polished by the overriding Merced Glacier. Both rock masses are **roches moutonnées** of gigantic size. Discontinuous master joints have given rise to successive terraces. Illilouette Ridge in the background. Photograph by François Matthes.

Plate 16. Front view of Mount Broderick and Liberty Cap. The sheer, hackly faces on the lee (pluck) sides were subjected to the quarrying action of the Merced Glacier. The V-shaped cleft between them was gouged out along a narrow zone of shattered rock. An inclined shear zone traversing the mass of Liberty Cap is readily traced by the bushes that have found a roothold in it. At the base of Mount Broderick, two horizontal shear zones give rise to successive rock benches. Photograph by François Matthes.

Plate 17. Profile of cliff at Glacier Point. The man at the top stands on Photographer's Rock, the smaller of two overhanging slabs at the brink of the great precipice. In the background is Half Dome. Photograph by A. C. Pillsbury.

Plate 18. View from Glacier Point, looking toward the Yosemite Falls and into the hanging valley of Yosemite Creek. This is the most striking example in the Yosemite region of a hanging valley with a waterfall leaping from its mouth. In the left foreground is the overhanging rock of Glacier Point. Photograph by Ansel Adams.

Plate 19. North face of Glacier Point in winter. The diagonal rock faces owe their existence to master joints. The Ledge Trail ascends the terrace directly below the small avalanche which is seen just left of the center of the photograph. Glacier Point was overridden during the period of maximum glaciation. Photograph by Ansel Adams.

Plate 20. The Three Brothers. This group is remarkable for its strongly asymmetric forms, which are due to the splitting of the rock along master joints. Photograph by Ansel Adams.

Plate 21. Sentinel Rock. The smooth, sheer front of this tall shaft is determined by nearly vertical joint fractures. Photograph by Ansel Adams.

Plate 22. View westward down the great corridor of Yosemite Valley. Sentinel Rock is in the left foreground; El Capitan, at the right in the middle distance. Photograph by Ansel Adams.

Plate 23. El Capitan, the great Rock Slides in the lower Yosemite chamber, and, seen against the cliffs at the extreme left, Ribbon Fall. El Capitan's bold profile is carved from exceptionally massive rock; but the cliffs to the left have crumbled because this rock was broken by many joint fractures. The Big Oak Flat Road descends into Yosemite Valley by switchbacks cut in the Rock Slides. Photograph by Ansel Adams.

Plate 24. The Cathedral Spires (left) and the Cathedral Rocks (center). The Cathedral Spires are among the frailest rock forms in the valley; the Cathedral Rocks are among the most massive. On the summits of the Cathedral Rocks lie glacial boulders which show that the ancient Yosemite Glacier once completely overwhelmed these rock masses. Photograph by Ansel Adams.

Plate 25. View southeastward across Yosemite Valley and into the hanging tributary valley of Bridalveil Creek. At the mouth of this truncated valley hangs Bridalveil Fall. Photographed by Ansel Adams.

Plate 26. The Royal Arches and the Washington Column surmounted by North Dome. The Royal Arches are sculptured in a slanting cliff 1,500 feet high. North Dome rises 2,000 feet higher. Photograph by Ansel Adams.

Plate 27. Stone Mountain, Georgia, a granite dome of the type so numerous and well developed in the Sierra Nevada of California.

Plate 28. Sentinel Dome, a typical dome of massive granite that owes its rounded form wholly to exfoliation—the casting off of successive shells. It has not been overridden by the glaciers of the Ice Age. Photograph by F. C. Calkins.

Plate 29. Front of Half Dome. The cliff came into existence first through the removal of thin rock sheets from a zone of nearly vertical joints, still visible in the shoulder at the northeast (left) end. The great monolith then began to exfoliate at its newly exposed surface, in plane shells curving under the old shells at the top. The old shells now form the overhanging cornice shown in plate 30. Photograph by François Matthes.

Plate 30. Northeast side of Half Dome. This view, taken from the subsidiary dome at the northeast end of the rock mass, reveals exfoliation on a gigantic scale. In the foreground is an old shell disintegrating, mainly as a result of daily temperature changes, into undecomposed granite sand. Photograph by F. C. Calkins.

Plate 31. Back of Half Dome. The curving back is enveloped by a single enormous shell. Its surface is not only striped with lichens, as are most cliffs in the Yosemite region, but it is fluted where rock grains washed down from the summit have worn furrows several feet deep. At the base are several imperfect arches produced by the dropping off of parts of shells. Photograph by Ansel Adams.

Plate 32. The Cascades. These cascades, tumbling and rebounding irregularly from a height of about 500 feet, contrast with the leaping falls that prevail in Yosemite Valley. Photograph by Ansel Adams.

Plate 33. Bridalveil Fall, typical of the free-leaping waterfalls of Yosemite Valley. Bridalveil Fall makes an unbroken descent of 620 feet over a vertical precipice. Photograph by Ansel Adams.

Plate 34. Vernal Fall. The Merced River descends 317 feet by this fall, from the lowermost step of the Giant Stairway. The step is vertical and is composed of unfractured, massive granite. Photograph by Ansel Adams.

Plate 35. Illilouette Fall, a leaping fall of 370 feet. Ensconced in a deep gorge, it is visible from only a few directions and is relatively little known. Yet in point of volume it is the largest fall made by any of the Merced's tributaries. Photograph by Ansel Adams.

Plate 36. The Yosemite Falls, viewed from the Merced River. Upper Yosemite Fall, which descends 1,430 feet, is probably the highest leaping waterfall in the world. Lower Yosemite Fall, descending 320 feet, is twice as high as the Niagara Falls. The total descent of the two falls and the intermediate cascade is 2,565 feet. To the right of Upper Yosemite Fall, partly detached from the cliff, is the pinnacle known as the Lost Arrow, about 1,500 feet high. Photograph by Ansel Adams.

Plate 37. The cliff of Upper Yosemite Fall and part of the gorge below. The stream has dried up and the fall disappeared because of long-continued drouth. The cave at the foot of the cliff appears as a dark line. Photograph by François Matthes.

Plate 38. The cave at the foot of Upper Yosemite Fall, as exposed in late summer when the fall has disappeared. Photograph by François Matthes.

Plate 39. Joint blocks loosened by frost. The rock mass shown here was quarried by the glacier from the head wall of the cirque above Ostrander Lake. Frost has since split it into minor blocks. Photograph by François Matthes.

Plate 40. Glacier polish on floor of massive granite. The surface of the rock is scaling in places as a result of weathering, but much of the polish is still in place and is likely to endure for a long time. Photograph by G. K. Gilbert.

Plate 41. One of the lateral moraines of the later (Wisconsin) glaciation on the north side of the Little Yosemite Valley. The moraine is composed mainly of angular blocks torn by the glacier from cliffs farther up the Little Yosemite and in the upper Merced Canyon. The Sunrise Trail follows the sandy hollow between this moraine and the next higher. Photograph by François Matthes.

Plate 42. One of the best-preserved moraines of the earlier (El Portal) series. It is below the Wawona Road, south of Turtleback Dome. Most of the older moraines have long since lost their ridge forms and can be identified with certainty only by the character of their constituent rock materials. Photograph by François Matthes.

Plate 43. Glacial boulder perched on a 5-foot pedestal, which is the highest pedestal in the Yosemite region. It is on the mountain west of Upper Yosemite Fall. The pedestal is composed of slabs of the local rock—remnants of concentric shells that formerly enveloped a large part of the summit. Photograph by F. C. Calkins.

Plate 44. Erratic boulder at the base of Sentinel Dome. A row of such boulders marks the highest level reached by the ice in the vicinity of Glacier Point. The sole remnants of a very ancient moraine, the rest of which has long since disappeared, they are believed to record a stage of glaciation that antedated the El Portal stage, and has been named the Glacier Point stage. The boulder shown here was angular when it was deposited by the ice; it has become rounded through long-continued exfoliation. Photograph by F. C. Calkins.

Plate 45. Large erratic boulder on the slope of Moraine Dome, above Little Yosemite. The boulder is composed of Cathedral Peak granite, readily recognized by the big feldspar crystals projecting from its surface. It measures 12 by 6 by 5 feet, and is perched on a pedestal 3 feet high. The pedestal consists of a remnant of a shell detached by exfoliation from the body of the dome. The noted geologist Grove Karl Gilbert is standing by the boulder. Photograph by E. C. Andrews.

Plate 46. Weather pits in slab on summit of North Dome. These pits have been formed entirely since the earlier ice passed over and smoothed the crown of the dome. The ice of the later glacial stage did not reach this level. Several of the weather pits shown here have expanded until they coalesce. Others are about to coalesce, the partitions between them having already partly broken down. Photograph by François Matthes.

Plate 47. Wall of aplite on Moraine Dome. This vertical dike has remained standing because the aplite disintegrates much more slowly than the surrounding granite. The height of the wall (7 ft.) affords a minimum measure of the depth to which the granite has been stripped since the earlier ice passed over and smoothed the crown of the dome. Photograph by G. K. Gilbert.

Plate 48. Mirror Lake. The basin of this lake is not of glacial origin, but was formed some time after the Ice Age by great rock avalanches thrown down, presumably, by an earthquake. The lake is rapidly being encroached upon by the expanding delta of Tenaya Creek. The mountain reflected in the lake is Mount Watkins, the El Capitan of Tenaya Canyon. Photograph by Ansel Adams.

Plate 49. Yosemite Valley, from the Wawona Road. At the left is El Capitan; at the right, the Cathedral Rocks and Bridalveil Fall. Through the portal between the opposing rock masses is the upper or main chamber of Yosemite Valley. In the foreground is the lower chamber, flanked at the left by the Rock Slides. Photograph by Ansel Adams.

Plate 50. Hetch Hetchy Valley before it was transformed into a reservoir. Though only half as long and half as wide, the Hetch Hetchy resembles the Yosemite in general form as well as in cliff sculpture. At the right is Kolana Rock; at the left, a cliff resembling El Capitan. Photograph by François Matthes.

1 The Sierra Nevada

Were we to start from San Francisco in an air-plane and fly due east, we would pass first over the wooded crests of the Coast Ranges; next over the broad, level expanse of the Great Valley of California, checkered with irrigated fields, vineyards, and orchards; and then, after a flight of about a hundred miles, we would come to a huge mountain barrier, stretching north and south at right angles to our course and rising in a long, gradual slope to a resplendent row of snow-flecked peaks. This is the Sierra Nevada, the longest, the highest, and the grandest single mountain range in the United States.[1]

---

[1] The Spanish word "sierra" means literally "saw" and is by the Spaniards commonly applied to serrate mountain ranges; "sierra nevada" therefore means "snowy mountain range." The great California range now known as the Sierra Nevada was first sighted, described, and placed on a map by the Franciscan missionaries Francisco Garcés and Pedro Font, who accompanied the Anza expedition that marched overland from Sonora, Mexico, in 1775–1776, for the purpose of founding San Francisco. "Looking to the northeast from a point just south of Suisun Bay," wrote Font in his diary on April 2, 1776, "we saw an immense treeless plain into which the water spreads widely, forming several low islets; at the opposite end of this extensive plain, about 40 leagues off, we saw a snow-covered mountain range

The Sierra Nevada may be likened to a gigantic ocean wave rolling landward from the west. Rising in a grand sweep from the trough of the Great Valley, this giant wave culminates in a somewhat sinuous snowy top, as in a foam crest, and with its precipitous front threatens the low-lying deserts to the east. At its northern end the wave splits into three lesser crests,[2] the altitudes there ranging between 7,000 and 9,000 feet; but throughout the greater part of its length it has a single clean-cut crest line, rising southward by degrees to 13,000 feet, opposite Mono Lake, and reaching a climax in the 14,000-foot peaks about Mount Whitney. Still farther south the range declines to 6,000 feet and, curving toward the west, merges with the Coast Ranges near Tehachapi Pass. So strongly asymmetric is the Sierra Nevada that its crest line is for the most part within a few miles of its eastern base but thirty to seventy miles from its western base.

Share with me, in imagination, the thrilling experience of an ascent of the range, from its parched western foothills, where the scanty grass assumes the lush green of springtime for only a few weeks, and wears the golden tint of autumn for the rest of the year; up through the less desolate chaparral belt, where the slopes are densely clad with small-leaved, impenetrable bushes; up into the majestic forests of the middle slope, where, favored by summer warmth and prodigious winter snows, pine and fir and cedar lift their tops 200 to 250 feet above the ground; to the zone of superlative tree growth, where the columnar sugar pine, with its twenty-inch cones, vies in height with the thousand-year-old sequoia; still farther up, into the lodgepole belt, where the snows linger until midsummer, and where tree stature dwindles; into the timber-line zone, with its recumbent dwarf trees, its emerald short-grass meadows, and its rock-bound sapphire lakelets; and finally up the stark summit peaks, in whose deeply sculptured recesses snow fields and tiny glaciers blaze under a sky of immaculate blue. Thence one may look northward and southward over an array of boldly carved, snow-flecked peaks and eastward over the empty vastness of the "land of little rain."

In this imaginary traverse of the range we have come through the famous gold belt of the lower western slope, where the forty-niners might make a fortune in a day and gamble it away in a night; where the town of Columbia, now dead and shuttered, once aspired to become the national capital; where there developed three of this country's greatest humorists—Mark Twain, Bret Harte, and Bill Nye.

[una gran sierra nevada], which seemed to me to run from south-southeast to north-northwest." *The Anza Expedition of 1775–1776: Diary of Pedro Font* (ed. by Frederick J. Teggart), Publications of the Academy of Pacific Coast History, Vol. III, No. 1 (1913), pp. 84–85.

[2] The minor ranges (named from west to east) Clermont Hill, Grizzly Mountain, and Diamond Mountain.

We are strongly tempted to leave our route and follow a winding million-dollar highway to a reservoir at great altitude—a lake held together by four great dams and fed through a tunnel thirteen miles long—and then to follow the hard-worked water as it plunges by thousand-foot steps from powerhouse to powerhouse, to the foothills, there to be distributed through canals and ditches over what Clarence King so aptly termed the California exuberance of grainfield and orchard.

And there is also the irresistible urge to visit the tranquil aisles of the Mariposa Grove of Big Trees and continue to Yosemite Valley, whose El Capitan, Bridalveil Fall, and Half Dome are known to all the world, where half a million or more people flock each summer, even in years of financial depression, regaining physical vigor and serenity of mind in a region of rare scenic grandeur. And should we not, when so near it, ascend into the High Sierra, that remoter land of pinnacled crests, flashing snow fields, and gemlike lakes which Californians in their wisdom have closed to industrial enterprise, that it may forever remain in its glorious virgin wildness, a delight to all who have the eye to see and the soul to know its grandeur.

Our imaginary visit to the range is unusual in that we have a purpose over and above the quest for beauty and refreshment. The fullest appreciation of any landscape comes only when one is alive to its meaning also. Surely in the sublime Yosemite region this truth should provide an absorbing, even exciting, intellectual adventure. We seek an answer to the question: By what circumstances did the Yosemite become endowed with scenic grandeur so exceptional that men have termed it "the Incomparable Valley"?

To answer this question has been the author's pursuit through years that have lengthened into decades; and to share with others the answers he has found has been his greatest happiness. But he begs that the reader be patient if the answer is not forthcoming in the first chapter of the book, or in the second, or even in the third. For so vast is the Sierra Nevada—a single range, yet with a magnitude comparable to an entire mountain system—that we can hardly hope to comprehend many features, including Yosemite Valley, which, however extraordinary in themselves, are actually but details in its mighty slopes, until we first appreciate the broad relationships of the entire range, lest we miss the forest for the trees. Clearly, our first concern is with the Sierra Nevada itself: its scenic features and their origin.

There could scarcely be a more complete antithesis between contiguous features of the earth's surface than there is between the Sierra Nevada and the lowlands that adjoin it on each side—the Great Valley of California and the Great Basin of Nevada and Utah. As compared with the lofty range, the Great Valley of California is an almost feature-less plain. More than one-third of its total area—nearly 3,000 square miles—is less than 100 feet above sea level. Upon this plain, which is on the whole arid, owing to prolonged summer heat and drought, issue the numerous snow-fed rivers that descend from the western flank of the range. The life-giving waters of these rivers have made possible the development of the great farming and fruit-growing industries for which the valley is famous.

The Great Basin, which begins at the east foot of the Sierra Nevada, is a lowland of a wholly different type—a vast province of sagebrush plains interspersed with sharp-crested mountain ranges. Though low in comparison with the Sierra and the other highlands that enclose it, its plains lie mostly at altitudes between 3,000 and 6,000 feet, and its ranges attain 10,000 to 13,000 feet. The Great Basin is characterized by saline lakes and salt-encrusted desert basins (playas) in which nearly all its streams terminate, the water evaporating into the thirsty air and leaving its salt content behind. Great Salt Lake, in Utah, is the largest and best known of these briny desert lakes, but there are many lesser ones. Several lie close to the Sierra Nevada and receive the waters from its eastern front. Among them are Mono Lake, directly east of the Yosemite region, and Owens Lake, southeast of Mount Whitney.

To one who stands on the crest of the Sierra Nevada and views the well-watered and forest-clad range, and then the vast desert wastes that stretch to the east, the contrast is impressive. Why is this mountain country so well favored by nature and the lowland to the east so neglected and desolate? The reason is that the Sierra Nevada, like every other mountain range of great height and extent, is itself a "climate maker." In large measure it is the author of its own weather conditions and controls those of the regions to leeward. Lying parallel to the Pacific Coast, it forms a barrier over which the vapor-laden winds from the ocean must rise. As they are forced up to high levels, they are chilled and discharge their condensed water vapor. Most of this precipitation falls in winter, in the form of snow, the summers being remarkably dry.

The abundance of winter snows in the Sierra Nevada is not generally known. Actually, they exceed those in any other part of the United States, save the Olympic Mountains, the northern Cascade Range, and possibly a limited area in the northern Rockies. According to the records of the United States Weather Bureau, the annual snowfall at stations on the Southern Pacific Railroad, at altitudes between 6,000 and 7,000 feet, totals 30 to 40 feet in depth. In some winters it reaches a total of 60 feet. A depth of as much as 20 feet of snow has been reported in a single month, and often there are 10 or 12 feet of snow on the ground at one

time. The heavy precipitation on the Sierra Nevada explains the barrenness of the Great Basin. The air currents are wrung dry as they pass
over the range.

Even the Sierra Nevada is not equally favored with moisture in all
parts. The bulk of the snow and rain falls on the west slope between the
4,000-foot and 9,000-foot levels. The foothills and lower slope partake
in large measure of the semiarid conditions that prevail in the Great
Valley; the higher peaks and crests also are relatively dry, the air currents having discharged most of their vapor content before reaching those
heights. The High Sierra, it is true, retains its white garb much longer
in spring and summer than the middle slope, but that is due primarily
to the lingering cold, which retards the melting. The east front of the
range, also, is arid in comparison with the west slope.

Heavy winter snows effectually preclude permanent settlement of
the higher parts of the range. The few forest rangers and employees of
hydroelectric companies who remain on duty in winter have to use snow-
shoes or skis for travel. To prevent its tracks from being blocked by snowdrifts and avalanches the Southern Pacific Railroad finds it necessary at
the higher levels to maintain many miles of snowsheds built of heavy
timber.

The summers in the Sierra Nevada are extremely dry. Rainless periods
of two or three months are common, though occasional thunderstorms
occur, especially in the High Sierra; camping without tents is therefore
a common practice. So enjoyable and salubrious is the summer climate
in the higher parts of the range that they have become a mecca for vaca-
tion seekers. Besides the half million or more people who annually visit
Yosemite National Park, thousands flock to the other portions of the
range that are now accessible by highways.

Because of the unequal distribution of snow and rain on the Sierra
Nevada, and the wide range in temperature from the torrid foothills
to the wintry crest, there are several distinct climatic belts, or zones, each
with its characteristic forms of vegetation and animal life. These zones
are broadest and most distinct on the western flank of the range.

The semiarid foothill belt, hot and dry in summer but rainy in winter,
corresponds to what biologists term the Upper Sonoran life zone. Its
characteristic vegetation is thin grass, bushy chaparral, and scattered
groups of live oaks and digger pines. Between altitudes of 3,000 and
4,000 feet it merges with the great forest belt, or transition life zone,
which has a more genial climate in summer and receives considerable
snow in winter. In the midst of its stately forests of yellow pine, sugar
pine, incense cedar, Douglas fir, and white fir stand scattered groves of
giant sequoias.

At altitudes ranging from 6,000 to 7,000 feet begins the Canadian life zone, characterized mainly by stands of lodgepole pine, Jeffrey pine, and red fir. It is sought in summer for its delightful climate but shunned in winter because of its frigidity. Toward the 9,000-foot level the silver pine and mountain hemlock appear, and the Hudsonian life zone sets in. In this picturesque timber-line belt only the hardiest species of trees can thrive. At its extreme upper limit, between 10,000 and 11,000 feet, the white-bark pine occurs in curiously storm-twisted, recumbent, or prostrate forms.

Above the timber line, in the alpine life zone, the mountainsides and peaks rise essentially bare of vegetation. Here, from altitudes of 11,000 feet upward, the precipitation, even in summer, consists largely of snow or hail, and the temperature in the shade seldom rises much above the freezing point. Snowdrifts abound until far into midsummer, and perennial bodies of old, hard snow and even small glaciers linger in the shaded, steep-walled recesses among the higher peaks.

The gentle inclination of the western slope of the Sierra Nevada has received much comment. It is usually stated to average 2°, which seems surprisingly low for a mountain mass of imposing height. A slope of 2° descends at a rate of 185 feet per mile, or, in engineering terms, it has a grade of 3.5 per cent. That is less than the maximum grade (4 per cent) that is regarded as allowable for a main-line railroad. Actual measurements show that in the northern half of the range the inclination is even less than 2°. In the latitude where the Southern Pacific crosses the range the inclination is only 1° 35', which is equivalent to a grade of 2.8 per cent. No wonder the Southern Pacific is able to make the ascent without resorting to complicated loops and switchbacks, for it follows a divide between two canyons.

But there are no railroad grades on the lofty and less well-known southern half of the Sierra Nevada. From the western foothills to Mount Whitney on the crest line, the slope rises 14,050 feet in a distance of forty-five miles. Its inclination averages 3° 23', or nearly 6 per cent. Even this figure is not strictly representative of actual conditions, for the Sierra there bears a second crest about a dozen miles west of Mount Whitney. From the foothills to this second crest, known as the Great Western Divide, the inclination is 4° 30', or nearly 8 per cent. Nor does the range there slope smoothly to the level of the Great Valley; it breaks off so abruptly that not even a foot trail can be laid without numerous zigzags. The much-quoted figure of 2°, therefore, is by no means representative of the range as a whole.

The Sierra Nevada, geologists are agreed, consists essentially of a single, huge, massive block of the earth's crust lying in a tilted position, with its eastern edge raised to great height and its broad surface slanting westward to the Great Valley of California. The eastern side of the block, exposed as the result of a tremendous dislocation of the crust, rises like an imposing façade thousands of feet above the Owens Valley and the other lowlands farther to the north. The Sierra does not owe its great elevation to a wrinkling of the crust, as do many other ranges. In the eastern half of California, apparently, the crust was too rigid and brittle to yield by bending and folding to the push and heave of disturbances within the earth, but cracked into angular blocks and slabs, like a badly laid cement sidewalk.

The entire Great Basin, which extends eastward from the Sierra Nevada for some four hundred miles, as far as the Wasatch Range behind Salt Lake City, is similarly broken into angular blocks. The upheaved blocks stand out as detached mountain ranges, and the sunken blocks, buried under great thicknesses of rock waste washed down from the heights, give rise to basin-shaped valleys from which the waters find no egress to the sea. These basin ranges trend toward the north, roughly parallel to one another and to the Sierra Nevada. That great range is, in fact, the westernmost of the entire system, and the Wasatch is the easternmost.

Yet to place the Sierra Nevada in the same category with the basin ranges would hardly be justifiable, for, compared with even the largest— the Inyo Range, to the east of the Owens Valley—it is in truth a mammoth range. Many of the basin ranges are not as long as the Sierra is broad, and they average only about half as high. Four hundred and thirty miles long and forty to eighty miles broad, the Sierra Nevada stands, over long stretches, 8,000 to 11,000 feet high above its eastern base and 13,000 to 14,000 feet above its western foothills. Not only does it bear the summit of greatest altitude south of Alaska—Mount Whitney, 14,496 feet above sea level—but it stands highest above its immediate base. The Sierra Nevada is, in fact, the greatest block range within the continental United States; it is the greatest continuous mountain range of any type in the country.

The colossal proportions of the Sierra Nevada are best appreciated if comparisons are made with other well-known western mountain ranges. The Rocky Mountains are popularly regarded as the great mountain bulwark of the Far West; but the Rockies in reality comprise a vast system of ranges and groups of mountains, somewhat loosely woven together and interspersed with valleys and gaps. The largest mountain units in that system are less than two hundred miles long—less than half as long as the Sierra Nevada. And the 14,000-foot peaks of the Rocky Mountains rise only about 7,000 feet above the Great Plains, which attain elevations of from 5,000 to 7,000 feet at the foothills; but the highest peaks of the Sierra Nevada tower 10,000 and even close to 11,000 feet above the Great Valley of California.

A more formidable competitor might be sought in the Cascade Range. It is true that this range far outstrips the Sierra Nevada in total length. Including the northernmost part, which projects across the Canadian boundary line, it is seven hundred miles long—two hundred seventy miles longer than the Sierra Nevada. But the Cascade Range is not a solid, unbroken mountain barrier. It is cut in two by the deep and broad gorge of the Columbia River, and its southern half, in Oregon and northern California, is dismembered by the canyons of the cross-flowing Klamath and Pit rivers. No river has cut a swath across the Sierra Nevada. To find an unbroken range of greater length than the Sierra Nevada, one must look beyond the limits of the continental United States.

The Sierra Nevada, because of its continuity, height, and ruggedness, has always presented a formidable obstacle to east-west travel. The few available gaps in its sawtooth crest are neither deep nor accessible. Donner Pass, through which the Southern Pacific Railroad is laid, has an altitude of about 7,000 feet. Tioga Pass, familiar to motorists as the picturesque notch on the route from the Yosemite to Mono Lake, has an altitude of 9,941 feet. It is rarely free from snow before July. Thence southward to Walker Pass is a stretch of 180 miles without a single pass available for vehicular traffic—only steep pack trails which climb to 11,000 feet and in places even thread their laborious way at heights exceeding 12,000 feet.

Small wonder that to the California-bound emigrants of the 'forties the Sierra Nevada was a formidable obstacle, more dreaded than the Rockies, the ranges of which could be by-passed or crossed at several well-worn trails. Those who chose to avoid the Sierra by going around its southern end had an exhausting journey through the furnace heat of the Mojave Desert. The majority, therefore, preferred to fight their way directly across the range, entering it by some gap or notch. But the Sierra Nevada offered no convenient gateway at any point. Nearly every possible crossing required a toilsome ascent, and even the lowest and easiest gaps led to long, roundabout routes among the rugged canyons and spurs of the western slope.

The memory of tragic disaster clings to several of these passes, especially Donner Pass, which became the main gateway for the west-bound wagon trains. This pass received its name from the ill-fated Donner Party, a group of Illinoisans who, overtaken at the lake east of the pass in October, 1846, by heavy winter snows, lost thirty-six of their members—men, women, and children—before, months later, succor reached them.

The Sierra Nevada is, indeed, not a simple, linear mountain range, but an uplifted and tilted segment of the earth's crust broad enough to bear on its back a whole system of linear mountain ranges. Nor are those superimposed ranges mere ridges a paltry thousand feet high. Many of them stand 3,000 to 4,000 feet above the adjoining valleys; not a few stand 5,000 feet high. Any one of the higher ranges, were it situated in a hilly or even moderately rugged part of the country, would dominate the landscape for miles around. But so numerous are the ranges on the sloping back of the Sierra block that many are as yet unnamed. These ranges are concentrated chiefly on the higher parts of the Sierra block in a belt ten to twenty miles wide, paralleling the main crest line. They are the boldly sculptured secondary crests that give the High Sierra, in the lofty central part of the Sierra Nevada, its sublime alpine aspect.

To mention but three of the High Sierra crests, there is, first, the Cathedral Range, in Yosemite National Park. Its summits, ascending in a series from Cathedral Peak (10,938 feet) to Mount Lyell (13,095 feet), rise from a minimum of 2,600 feet to a maximum of 4,000 feet above Tuolumne Meadows and Lyell Canyon. On the opposite (southwest) side the same peaks stand 4,000 to 5,000 feet above the upper Merced Canyon. On the Ritter Range, which is the prolongation of the Cathedral Range beyond the Park limits, Mount Ritter (13,161 feet) and Banner Peak (12,962 feet) stand 4,000 to 4,600 feet above the canyons of the Ritter Fork and the Middle Fork of the San Joaquin River. The total length of the Cathedral Range and the Ritter Range is twenty-two miles.

Farther south, in the center of the San Joaquin watershed, is Kaiser Ridge, which, though only about 10,000 feet high, looms 3,000 feet above Huntington Lake, that natural-looking reservoir at the head of a chain of powerhouses which has become a populous tourist center. On its north side Kaiser Ridge drops a full 4,000 feet to the valley of the South Fork of the San Joaquin. Continuous with it, but bending more to the southeast, is the spectacular LeConte Divide, whose 12,000-foot peaks rise nearly 4,000 feet above Goddard Canyon. And still farther southeast is the White Divide, which ends at Stewart Edward White's Tunemah Pass at an altitude of 10,900 feet, and a height of 4,900 feet above Simpson Meadow, on the Middle Fork of the Kings River. The over-all length of these connecting crests is about forty miles.

Farthest south is the Great Western Divide, which extends for thirty miles across Sequoia National Park and parts the waters flowing into the Kaweah River on the west from those flowing into the Kern River on the east. Viewed from Moro Rock, on the edge of the Giant Forest, its long row of spectacular 12,000-foot peaks, blazing with snow fields in midsummer, seems like a vista of the Swiss Alps. Many visitors mistake it for the main crest of the Sierra Nevada and try to identify Mount Whitney on it, not realizing that Mount Whitney and its 14,000-foot companions on the main crest stand fifteen miles farther east, hidden from view. The eye naturally singles out Sawtooth Peak (12,340 feet) as the most strikingly modeled of the whole array and it unconsciously seeks the deepest valley below that peak as the base from which to gauge its height; but few visitors, it is safe to say, would estimate the vertical distance from the top of Sawtooth to the Middle Fork of the Kaweah below to be a full 7,000 feet.

These spectacular crests in the High Sierra, though very impressive to the tiny human bipeds who crawl among them like ants, are, however, but corrugations on the surface of the Sierra block, details in its sculpture, which we are not yet ready to interpret. We must first consider how the Sierra block as a whole acquired its general form, its tilted attitude, and its imposing eastern façade.

The manner in which the originally flat Sierra block became tilted has long puzzled geologists. The Sierra Nevada is so large that no geologist can become familiar with all its features. Its outlines, inner structure, and surface sculpture vary from place to place, so that several equally competent geologists, examining different sections of the range, may arrive at somewhat different conclusions about certain aspects of its evolution.

On one point all geologists are agreed—that the dislocation of the earth's crust that caused the Sierra Nevada to stand so high and with so steep a front overlooking the country to the east was produced by slipping, or faulting, movements on a line of fractures reaching deep into the earth and extending for hundreds of miles along the eastern base of the range and around its curving southern portion, as far as the vicinity of Tehachapi Pass. The Sierra block and the contiguous valley block are conceived to have sheared past each other, the one upward, the other downward, relative to each other. (See fig. 2.)

The great eastern front of the Sierra Nevada is unquestionably a "fault escarpment," one of the grandest features of its kind in the world. The actual declivity of the escarpment at no point exceeds 25°; though this is a moderate angle, the effect upon a beholder stationed in the lowland to the east of the range is that of a formidable, well-nigh unscalable mountain wall. It is not merely the height of the escarpment that produces this effect, but the combination of great height and abrupt rise, without intermediate foothills or sprawling spurs, from the level plain at the base. Supremely impressive is the long, straight wall, facing the Owens Valley, that averages two miles in height. It is said that Albrecht

Penck, the dean of European geomorphologists, upon viewing this stupendous mountain front, was visibly affected by its grandeur and begged his guide to leave him for several hours that he might contemplate and study it in solitude.

The scientists who have come here, even from distant lands, have viewed the Sierra fault escarpment with awe, and have usually departed

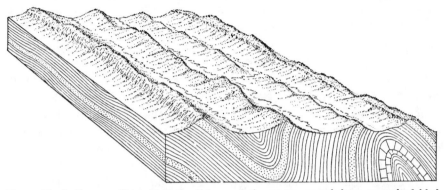

Fig. 1. Block diagram illustrating parallel mountain ranges carved from strongly folded strata. The ancient mountain ranges that occupied the place of the Sierra Nevada during the Cretaceous period were of this general type.

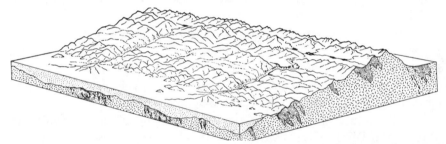

Fig. 2. Idealized representation of a portion of the tilted Sierra block, showing the "roots" of the ancestral Sierras penetrating deep into the granite; also longitudinal crests and valleys. Vertical scale exaggerated.

without offering more than a tentative explanation. The precise manner of the escarpment's origin is not patent at a glance. There are, indeed, several ways in which the dislocation could have taken place: (1) The Sierra block may have been thrust up by itself, leaving the country to the east lying low. (2) Both blocks may have risen, the Sierra block faster and to greater height than the valley block. (The lowest part of the Owens Valley has an elevation of 3,700 feet, and Mono Lake lies at an altitude of about 6,400 feet.) (3) The Sierra block and the valley block may first have risen together in one piece, as parts of a great bulge in the earth's crust that extended far to the east; then, when the bulge collapsed, the Owens Valley and the other valley lands may have sunk to their present levels, leaving the Sierra block standing high. (4) The Sierra block may have been thrust eastward and up onto the valley block, pushing the latter down.

The reader is invited to look at some of the factual evidence, which in large measure speaks for itself, and then he may form his own conclusions. Only, he must do so cautiously, remembering that geology is a fast-progressing science and that the convictions we cherish today may have to be modified or even abandoned tomorrow, in the light of new discovery.

Much of the uncertainty in regard to the nature of the faulting movements that have taken place at the eastern base of the Sierra Nevada is due to the fact that most of the fractures are concealed from view. So much time has elapsed since the last major faulting movements that the sheer cliffs produced by them have long since crumbled back to slopes, and the mountain front throughout its length has become gashed by canyons. The fractures at the base of the range are buried under accumulations of rock debris, under masses of gravel swept out of the canyons by torrential floods, and under lava, cinders, and pumice ejected by volcanoes that spouted through the cracks.

Fortunately, however, renewed faulting on a small scale has occurred in fairly recent times, so recently that the resulting little "scarps" are still fresh and easily recognized. Most of them are only 10 or 20 feet high, but some measure 40 to 100 feet, and have the aspect of smooth, sheer cliffs at the immediate base of the range, or of steep bluffs where they cut across masses of loose rock debris or gravel. Some of the lava flows in the Owens Valley are broken by parallel faults, and "step down" 10 or 15 feet at each fracture. One small volcanic cone, seven miles to the south of Big Pine, is neatly cut in two by one of these recent faults.

Perhaps the reader would prefer not to have his attention drawn to these fresh breaks in the earth's crust, while he is pleasantly touring up the Owens Valley and northward to Mono Lake, feeling reasonably secure in the thought that the solid-looking mountains have been standing for ages and are not likely to heave, or fall, just when one is passing. For it is disquieting to reflect that even these little scarps, that seem insignificant in a landscape framed by mile-high peaks, were produced instantaneously by a sudden snapping of the earth's crust accompanied by an earthquake. Many minor faulting movements have taken place in recent geologic time and right up to the present—evidence that the stresses within the earth which have built the Sierra Nevada have by no means spent themselves.

Detailed investigations have shown that the Sierra block is bounded along its eastern base not by one continuous, sweeping master fracture,

but by a multitude of short fractures, each only a few miles, or less than
a mile, long, and in an irregular zigzag pattern. Such fractures outline
individual spurs and reëntrants in the mountain front. The same is true
at the base of the Inyo Range and the White Mountains, which comprise the northern portion of that range. Many of these fractures can be
traced for some distance into the lowland between the two mountain
blocks, but in the massive bodies of those blocks they die out. The low-

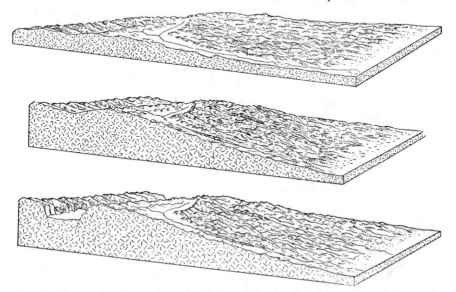

Fig. 3. Diagrammatic cross sections, showing stages in the rise of the Sierra block and the
down-faulting of the Mono Lake region.
 (1) Sierra Nevada before major uplift; (2) Sierra Nevada after major uplift; (3) Sierra
Nevada after down-faulting of the Mono Lake region.

land is crisscrossed by innumerable intersecting fractures. It is broken
into a mosaic of small angular blocks, some of which stand out as low
ridges or tablelands, while the intermediate sunken blocks form narrow
valleys or enclosed basins. The country lying between the Sierra and
the Inyo Range and extending northward to Mono Lake may be said
to repeat the structure of the Great Basin on a small scale.

North of Mono Lake the Sierra front is extremely irregular; long
spur ranges branch from it, mostly in northerly directions, while the
main mountain mass trends northwestward. All those spur ranges, which
are not unlike huge splinters torn from the side of the Sierra block, are
bounded by faults, and small fresh scarps occur here and there along
their bases. Lake Tahoe occupies a basin between the Sierra block and
one of those great splinters—the Carson Range. Its great depth, 1,685
feet, cannot be accounted for either by stream cutting or glacial erosion,
but must have been produced by the subsidence of an earth block. The

dislocations occurred long ago, and the fault scarps have lost their characteristic forms, but at the eastern base of the Carson Range, near Genoa, Nevada, are fresh cliffs 40 to 50 feet high that still retain the vertical grooves and the polish (slickensides) produced by recent slipping movements under great pressure.

Now it is significant that the fresh fault scarps occur only locally, at intervals along the four hundred miles of the Sierra front. If they were in a continuous line, one would be justified in regarding them as evidence of a recent uplift of the entire Sierra block. But the scarps are widely scattered, and wholly absent over long stretches; moreover, they differ greatly in height. It therefore seems far more probable that they were produced by the settling of relatively small local blocks in the mosaic of the badly shattered valley lands.

That it is the valley lands that are sinking and not the Sierra Nevada that is rising is indicated also by two other facts. First, opposite several of the fresh scarps at the base of the Sierra front the lowland slants perceptibly toward the foot of the range, and there is either an area of wet, marshy land or a shallow lake. Examples are Honey Lake, at the extreme northern end of the Sierra escarpment; the marshes in Carson Valley which lie directly beneath fresh fault cliffs at the base of the Carson Range; Mono Lake, the waves of which beat against the foot of the mountain wall; the wet, slanting meadows to the north of Big Pine; and Owens Lake, which hugs the base of a 7,000-foot escarpment and is deepest near its western shore, in spite of the quantities of rock waste that are being washed into it from the precipitous mountain front.

Second, in 1872, when the famous Owens Valley earthquake took place—a catastrophe which destroyed the village of Lone Pine and killed many of its inhabitants—an east-facing scarp 8 to 20 feet high was formed, and 60 feet to the east of it, a west-facing scarp 6 to 10 feet high. Between the opposing scarps the ground sank. The resulting strip of low, marshy land with ponds in it long remained a noticeable feature in the valley, but its outlines are now dim, for the scarps consisted merely of soft mud that had accumulated in an ancient lake—the large Owens Lake of glacial times—and they have gradually slumped to gentle slopes.

The main east-facing scarp near Lone Pine is not at the foot of the Sierra Nevada but five miles east of it, at the front of a block within the Owens Valley—the block that bears those queer little mountains known as the Alabama Hills.[3] Directly west of Lone Pine, the scarp is

---

[3] Many dramatic scenes for moving pictures have been "shot" among the fantastically sculptured granite crags of the Alabama Hills. The Alabama Hills, indeed, have become a favorite location for motion-picture companies. They afford a wonderful array of weird rock forms for desert foregrounds, and the Sierra Nevada, resplendent in its mantle of winter snow, satisfactorily represents the Himalayas in the background.

remarkably well preserved where it crosses the broad gravel wash that once was the bed of Lone Pine Creek. The stream, having found a new course through a notch in the Hills, no longer floods the wash, and since heavy showers are rare the scarp has remained almost unchanged since the faulting took place in 1872. If you have never seen a fresh earthquake scarp, here is an excellent opportunity to observe one at close range.

As we have seen, the recent small dislocations along and near the eastern base of the Sierra Nevada were produced not by a rise of the mountain block but by subsidence of the valley blocks. There remains the question: How was the imposing front of the range produced—the great Sierra escarpment, which varies in height from 2,000 feet at the north to 7,000 feet at Owens Lake? Was it by uplift of the Sierra block, the Owens Valley remaining at its present low level; or was it by the sinking of the valley block, the Sierra remaining standing with its previously attained height; or was it a combination of both kinds of movement?

The answer is found in the positions of the deposits of ice-borne debris (moraines) built by the glaciers which occupied the canyons in the escarpment during the Ice Age. The moraines indicate not only the character of the faulting movements but the approximate time of the movements.

The moraines are ridges composed of rock debris that accumulated along the flanks of the glaciers as it was released by the melting ice. They are typically sharp-crested and extend unbroken for miles, almost as regular in form as railroad embankments. The so-called Ice Age consists really of four successive glaciations, or glacial stages, separated by long intervals of approximately normal climate. As a consequence, there are four sets of moraines differing greatly in antiquity and degree of preservation. The moraines of the latest glaciation have remarkably perfect forms, but the moraines of the preceding glaciations, which are hundreds of thousands of years old, are poorly preserved and relatively obscure, the more so the older they are. The oldest are in large part destroyed but they are still recognizable in spots.

From the mouths of many canyons the sharp-crested moraines of the latest glaciation extend into the lowland to the east of the range. They show by their positions that when the last glaciers advanced the canyons had already attained their present depth. Some of these moraines "step down" abruptly 50 feet or more where they cross the fault line at the foot of the range. In those places only one small dislocation has occurred within, perhaps, the last 25,000 years. Few of the older moraines extend into the lowland. Most of them are cut off at the fault line, in some instances at heights of 1,000 to 1,500 feet. Thus we know that faulting movements of that order of magnitude have taken place since those moraines were deposited—that is, during the last 500,000 years.

The oldest moraines, which may be from 750,000 to 1,000,000 years old, lie not in the canyons or at their mouths but high on their shoulders, thousands of feet above the lowland. The finest example is the partially disintegrated moraine lying on the mountains west of McGee Canyon. It terminates at the brink of the escarpment, 3,000 feet above Long Valley. To judge from its gentle slope, moreover, this ancient moraine was built by a glacier that lazily wended its way through a rather flat, shallow valley high on the Sierra block. McGee Canyon evidently had not yet been cut. But this implies that there was as yet no escarpment. It is, then, an inescapable conclusion that the major faulting movements did not begin until after the first glaciation—that is, roughly, less than 750,000 years ago. The great Sierra escarpment, accordingly, appears to be only about 750,000 years old.

But how was it formed? Did the Sierra rise 3,000 feet, or did Long Valley drop 3,000 feet? The ancient McGee Moraine[4] is of about the same dimensions as the moraines of the later glaciations, and that fact, together with similar evidence from other parts of the range, warrants the inference that during the first glaciation the Sierra Nevada was about as extensively mantled with glaciers as during the later glaciations. That, however, could not have been true unless at that time the range was already as high as it was during the later glaciations. It might have been somewhat lower, but it could not have been 3,000 feet lower, for then its summit would have lain below the level of the snow line and would have borne no glaciers. The three main peaks at the head of McGee Canyon—Red and White Mountain (12,840 feet), Mount Crocker (12,448 feet), and Mount Stanford (12,826 feet)—would have stood only 9,000 to 10,000 feet high, yet from detailed glaciologic studies it is evident that in this part of the Sierra Nevada the snow line during glacial times never lay much below 11,000 feet.

It follows from this, inevitably, that the Sierra Nevada could not have risen 3,000 feet since the first glaciation. The 3,000-foot escarpment below the ancient McGee Moraine could not have been produced by uplift of the Sierra block; it must have been produced by subsidence of the adjoining valley block. It is, of course, probable that the successive downward movements of the lowlands were accompanied by upward jerks of the mountain mass, but, if so, the jerks were relatively small and did not materially increase the height of the range.

Evidence at other points along the Sierra front tends to confirm these conclusions. Wherever it has been examined, the escarpment appears

[4] This venerable ridge of disintegrating glacial boulders is sufficiently impressive to be worthy of a pilgrimage, not only by students of geology but by all who wish to comprehend the mode of evolution of the Sierra Nevada. The moraine can be reached by an easy climb from Convict Lake.

to owe its great height primarily to the sinking of the adjacent valley lands rather than to uplift of the Sierra Nevada. And that interpretation is consistent with the fact that the valley lands are shattered into innumerable small, angular blocks covered with volcanic materials that were erupted from vents along the fractures. By contrast, the Sierra Nevada exhibits no evidence of marked internal dislocations dating from the same period. Throughout the Ice Age, apparently, the weak valley blocks suffered deformation as they sank, while the mighty Sierra block remained standing, hardly changed in height and general form.

If the Sierra Nevada was about as high at the beginning of the first glaciation as it is now, how and when did it attain its great height? Nearly 60,000,000 years ago, at the beginning of the Cenozoic era (the era of mammals; see the table of geologic time divisions, p. 64), the Sierra region was a lowland forming the coastal margin of a continent that stretched far eastward. That there was no high mountain barrier at that time is to be inferred from the fact that lush vegetation requiring much rain existed a hundred miles inland. This the fossil plant remains indicate beyond possible doubt.

Then, during the Eocene epoch, the region was gradually uplifted and acquired a definite slant toward the coast, which was near the line of the present foothills. A low, broad mountain barrier arose as the result of a local uparching along the axis of the present Sierra-Cascade chain. During the Miocene epoch that barrier attained sufficient height to intercept a large share of the moisture blowing in from the Pacific, and as a result the country east of it became semiarid.

The end of the Miocene epoch and the beginning of the Pliocene were marked by many disturbances in the earth's crust. The Sierra was bowed up to a height of several thousand feet and acquired a strongly asymmetrical form, with a long western slope and a short, steep eastern slope. In the northern half of the range, fissures opened along the crest; from these fissures immense floods of steaming volcanic mud poured down both slopes. Fiery lava flows and showers of ash ejected from craters added to the sinister mantle of volcanic materials. Faulting movements accentuated the ruggedness of the eastern flank, especially north of Mono Lake. Several long spur ranges were blocked out there, and between one of these spurs, the Carson Range, and the main body of the Sierra Nevada, the deep basin of Lake Tahoe was formed by subsidence. Faults developed also along the western foothills, and the western slope became broken by successive abrupt steps. At the same time, presumably, the entire Central Valley of California sank below sea level.

There ensued an interval of relative quiet during which the erosive processes worked almost undisturbed. Long and fairly broad valleys were cut in the western slope of the Sierra Nevada, and short valleys of the same general type were carved in its steep eastern slope. Cottonwood Basin, to the south of Mount Langley, is representative of these eastward-draining valleys. It is only the upper half of such a valley left hanging at the brink of the Sierra escarpment. Mount Langley rises about 4,000 feet above it; it may reasonably be inferred, therefore, that during the Pliocene epoch Mount Langley and Mount Whitney towered 5,000 feet above the Owens Valley.

Toward the end of the Pliocene epoch, perhaps about 2,000,000 years ago, began those climactic earth movements that lifted the Sierra Nevada to its present great altitude. The range, however, did not rise alone. The country to the east rose with it, and Owens Valley came to lie 9,000 feet above sea level. This climax of crustal upwarping, moreover, happened just before the advent of the glaciers of the Ice Age. As the main peaks of the range rose higher, they eventually came to stand above the snow line. More snow accumulated on them each winter than could melt away in summer during this frigid period. Glaciers developed and flowed like sluggish streams down the valleys on both sides of the range. The ancient McGee Glacier was one of the ice streams on the east side of the divide. After this first stage of glaciation, or perhaps even before it was over, roughly 750,000 years ago, began the succession of faulting movements that resulted in the downthrow of the Owens Valley, Long Valley, and the other valleys farther north. So, to the roar of earthquakes and the thunder of falling rocks, the mighty Sierra escarpment was born. By the middle of the Ice Age the mountain front had attained three-fourths of its present height; and when the ice streams of the fourth and latest stage of glaciation advanced, the canyons in the escarpment had been cut to about their present depth, and the valley lands lay at nearly their present level. The rock floors had sunk below that level, but had become covered by stream and lake deposits, volcanic flows, cinders, and pumice. The sinking of the lowlands left the massive, rigid Sierra block standing in the form of a lofty, asymmetrical mountain range.

Ten turbulent master streams fed by great quantities of winter snow race down the western slope of the Sierra Nevada in roughly parallel courses. These rivers, in order from north to south, are the Feather, Yuba, American, Mokelumne, Stanislaus, Tuolumne, Merced, San Joaquin, Kings, and Kaweah. An eleventh master stream, the Kern, runs due south, lengthwise through the southern portion of the range, which is not tilted toward the west but declines southward, delimited on both sides by fault escarpments. Each of the master streams has trenched deeply into the body of the range, forming eleven steep-walled canyons.

Yet that is hardly an adequate description of the resulting sculpture of the Sierra block, for each master stream possesses at least a north fork, a middle fork, and a south fork, and the converging tributaries are themselves lusty rivers, fifty miles or more long, that have cut trenches proportionate to their eroding powers. Many of the forks in turn have lesser forks. So the western slope is dissected by an intaglio of ramifying canyons and gulches. Travel across the grain of the country is very wearisome; it requires climbing and descending thousands of feet in alternation, over and over again.

The main river canyons are by no means all of the same depth or the same type. In the northern part of the range, where the crest line averages 7,000 to 8,000 feet in altitude and the western slope is eighty miles long, the westward tilt of the Sierra block is so slight that the rivers cut with moderate vigor. Their canyons are for the most part only 1,500 to 2,500 feet deep; in only a few places do they attain depths of 3,000 feet. But farther south in the range, where the peaks of the main crest rise successively to altitudes of 12,000, 13,000, and 14,000 feet, and the western slope contracts to about sixty miles, the rivers had much steeper courses and trenched to correspondingly greater depths. Canyons 4,000 to 5,000 feet deep are not rare, and a few chasms attain depths of 6,000 and 7,000 feet, thus outrivaling the Grand Canyon of the Colorado River.

Nor are all the canyons noted for their scenery. The traveler on the Southern Pacific, who at Blue Canyon station has an opportunity to gaze into the depths of the canyon, is not likely to go into raptures. Blue Canyon is only 500 feet deep below the level of the railroad track. Its walls are of dull blue-black slate, so somber in tone that he may wonder why this has been called the "Range of Light." There are no striking rock forms, and not one spectacular peak is in sight. If the traveler has not previously beheld Yosemite Valley, the Kings River Canyon, or Mount Whitney, he may conclude that the beauty of the range has been grossly overrated.

Blue Canyon is, indeed, hardly more than a side gulch of the modest canyon of the North Fork of the North Fork of the American River. The canyons that traverse the northern part of the range, besides being low, suffered the dismal fate, toward the end of the Miocene epoch (see the table of geologic time divisions, p. 64) of being overwhelmed by successive floods of volcanic mud and showers of cinders from craters near the crest of the range. Those volcanic materials, accumulating bed upon bed, attained thicknesses of more than 1,000 feet, completely filled the valleys, and coalesced over the intervening divides. They obliterated the original stream-cut landscape, except for the highest peaks, and replaced it with a monotonous expanse of gray and brown rock that sloped to the foothills.

Upon this new surface the waters were reorganized in a new system of master streams, with many tributaries, and, as the range was bowed to greater and greater height, they became entrenched to progressively greater depth. They cut through the thick volcanic covering and into the slates, schists, and granitic rocks underneath. As a consequence, the northern canyons lack distinctive sculpture and are flanked by uplands with monotonous sky lines.

To the lover of glorious mountain scenery it seems providential that the devastating volcanic flows did not reach farther south, for had they spread another fifty miles there would be no Yosemite or Hetch Hetchy. Only the outermost fringes of the volcanic mantle overlap the western border of Yosemite National Park, on the uplands about Hetch Hetchy Valley and the lower Tuolumne Canyon, but they are so unobtrusive that only a geologist would notice them.

Near the western and northern borders of Yosemite National Park a change takes place also in the character of the country rock. The somber slates and schists make way for vast tracts of granite, and the granite, scraped bare of soil and thoroughly scrubbed by the ancient glaciers, reflects the sun's rays from myriads of milk-white feldspar crystals. Here, in truth, begins the "Range of Light."

The granite not only radiates brightness, but endows mountains and canyons with forms of striking individuality. At Hetch Hetchy the traveler who has just come up from the foothills, where slates and schists continue in a broad belt, suddenly finds himself in a landscape dominated by massive domes and sheer cliffs of granite 2,000 to 2,500 feet high. And if he happens to visit Hetch Hetchy in early summer, when the snow is melting fast, he will have the additional joy of beholding two exquisite but short-lived waterfalls, the Wapama, which churns through a tortuous cleft, and the Tueeulala, which makes a clear leap of 600 feet and a total descent of 1,000 feet.

Immediately above the Hetch Hetchy the uplands rise a full 3,000 feet higher, and there, between Rancheria Mountain on the north and Smith Peak on the south, begins that profound chasm, the Grand Canyon of the Tuolumne River. Throughout its fourteen miles the walls rise to heights of 4,000 to 5,200 feet. In depth, therefore, this chasm closely rivals the Grand Canyon of the Colorado River, but, what is more remarkable, it is less than half as wide. Whereas the Colorado's trench averages ten miles from rim to rim, and at no place in its deepest portion narrows to less than seven miles, the Tuolumne chasm through most of its course is but two miles wide. At the broadest place, between Rancheria Mountain and Double Rock, it measures only four miles from rim to rim. Its walls, consequently, are far steeper than those of the

Colorado's canyon. They are not broken by terraces, as is the latter, but rise with almost continuously sheer profiles.

It is noteworthy that the walls have shed little rock waste since the last glacier of the Ice Age left the chasm—that is, in about 15,000 to 20,000 years. Amazingly enduring they are, retaining, with only minor changes, the smooth contours which the grinding glaciers gave them. This strange fact leads to another which to a geologist seems even more remarkable. The walls, which are commonly described as sheer or perpendicular, are by no means vertical, but slope at angles averaging less than 45°, giving the chasm a pronounced V shape, very different from the spacious U shape which intensely glaciated canyons usually have. Yet the Tuolumne Glacier was by far the thickest and most powerful ice stream in the entire Sierra Nevada. During the earlier glaciations its volume was so great that large masses of ice spilled over the southern rim, invading the upland for several miles. On the northern side the ice completely engulfed the huge bulk of Rancheria Mountain. Even during the latest glaciation, when the ice streams throughout the range were shorter and thinner than their predecessors, the Tuolumne Glacier filled the chasm to the brink, as is attested by the lateral moraines it left in several places. The chasm by that time doubtless was cut substantially to its present depth. The latest Tuolumne Glacier thus attained a thickness of nearly 4,000 feet, an extraordinary thickness for a mountain glacier.

What quality of the granite prevented this exceptionally powerful ice stream from excavating a normal U-shaped canyon? And what quality of the rock enabled the walls to retain their glacial contours for thousands of years? To both questions the answer is to be found in the nature of the granite—not merely its hardness but its extreme solidity, due to the absence of fractures over long distances, both horizontally and vertically.

Granite (the term is here used for all types of granitic rocks) is a rock of igneous origin, which crystallized from hot, fluid magmas that welled up from below and invaded the hard rocks of the earth's crust. These magmas do not erupt at the surface of the earth but remain imprisoned several thousand feet beneath it. Bodies of granite are thus termed "batholiths" (deep-seated rocks). The appearance of granite at the surface, as in large areas of the Sierra Nevada, is due to the fact that the rocks of the crust that once overlay the batholith have been eroded by rain water, streams, glaciers, and other destructive agents. The time involved in such erosion aggregates millions of years.

A hot mass of magma cools first at its boundaries, in contact with the cold rocks of the earth's crust, where crystallization begins. The central and lower portions, meanwhile, are still fluid and continue to push up. The result is that the hardened marginal portions become rent by fractures. Some of the fractures open under tension but are immediately filled again by thinly fluid magma that shoots into them and, crystallizing, seals them up. Thus are formed the dikes (often miscalled "veins") of cream-colored or yellowish aplite that penetrate the granite in many places.

After all the granite has solidified, the formation of new joints may occur from entirely different causes. During periods of mountain building, earth movements may subject the rocks to bending, warping, and shearing stresses which again result in wholesale fracturing. The Sierra Nevada has experienced several successive uplifts and upwarpings. It is not surprising, therefore, that its rocks are crisscrossed by a multitude of fractures, large and small—some produced when the granite crystallized, others much later during times of crustal disturbance.

In some areas of the range the joints are sparse—tens, hundreds, even thousands of feet apart—and there the blocks of undivided rock between them are of immense size, monoliths in the true sense. This unusual condition may be due in part to the fact that all the joints are sealed by dikes of aplite, but it is undoubtedly due in part to the toughness of the rock masses which has enabled them to withstand powerful stresses. It is noteworthy that the lighter-colored, highly siliceous types of rock, which have the greatest tensile strength, generally have the most massive structure. The darker rocks—granodiorite, quartz diorite, diorite, and gabbro—which are more brittle, are more or less closely jointed.

Every joint is, of course, a plane of weakness in the rock. It is not only a plane of discontinuity, but also a potential avenue for percolating water, which is an insidious destructor of mountains, working from within. Entering at the surface charged with acids derived from decaying vegetal matter, it carries those acids deeper and deeper into the mass, decomposing the weaker minerals along its way. And when water freezes in the joints the powerful distending force of crystallizing ice tends to widen them and pry the blocks apart.

Closely jointed rock is far more vulnerable to the attacks of these destructive agencies than sparsely jointed rock. A cliff composed of small joint blocks gradually crumbles to an unimpressive slope. But a cliff made of a few monoliths hundreds or thousands of feet long, broad, and high will endure for incredibly long periods. The cliff dwellers in the arid Southwest realized this and felt safe in their abodes under towering cliffs of unfractured, massive sandstone.

The walls of the Tuolumne Canyon owe their remarkable preservation to the fact that they are composed of huge monoliths of granite.

The massive structure of the granite has prevented the Tuolumne Glacier from enlarging the chasm from a narrow V shape to a characteristic glacial U shape; for in hard rocks the glaciers pluck, or "quarry," out entire joint blocks. The process of erosion is naturally most effective where the rock is divided into small, light blocks. A glacier cannot dislodge monoliths hundreds or thousands of feet in extent. These it can only grind with the boulders and sand that are frozen in its base and flanks. In hard granites, such as those of the Sierra Nevada, however, the grinding process achieves small results. Glacier polish, though often considered to be an impressive evidence of a glacier's eroding power, really attests the opposite: the glacier's inability to erode efficiently in massive rock which it cannot quarry out block by block. By sandpapering and polishing massive granite, a glacier tends to produce an almost frictionless bed over which it glides.

Sparsely jointed, massive granite, because of its obdurate nature, has played a prominent role in the fashioning of the Sierra landscape. It accounts for the development of many unusual rock forms, and without it the Sierra would not possess its wealth of waterfalls. Massive granite endowed the Tuolumne Canyon not only with mile-high cliffs but with a smoothly sloping floor descending from its head near Glen Aulin to the depths of the constricted Muir Gorge, 2,000 feet below. Down that great incline the Tuolumne Glacier glided impotently during the waning stages of the Ice Age, and down it the Tuolumne River glides today in a lacelike sheet of frothy water, equally powerless to remodel the monolithic rock significantly. But at several spots in the smooth incline there are irregularities, trifling obstructions a few inches high, but so shaped that they violently deflect the rushing water in fountains of silvery spray. Carried over by their momentum, these fountains curve forward and descend in graceful arcs, thus producing the Waterwheel Falls, the rarest of all the varied types of waterfalls in the range.

The Yosemite is beyond compare the most ornately sculptured valley in the Sierra Nevada. What of its waterfalls, and the amazing array of contrasting forms that flank its sides, ranging from rounded domes to angular spurs and slender minarets? Does not the Sierra granite and the variations in its jointed structure supply clues to the origin of this unique assemblage? Assuredly it does, and furthermore, in becoming aware of the fact that erosion by streams and glaciers in the Sierra Nevada has been selective, controlled by the jointing of the granite, we can better understand how the Yosemite Valley itself was formed.

Farther south in the Sierra Nevada, none of the canyons equals the Yosemite in diversity of rock forms and wealth of waterfalls. Yet cliffs and domes of massive granite are by no means absent. The San Joaquin has its Balloon Dome; and Tehipite Valley, the Yosemite-like chamber in the canyon of the Middle Fork of the Kings River, is graced by the tall Tehipite Dome, which is regarded by many as the most superbly modeled of all the Sierra's domes. The South Fork Canyon, popularly known as the Kings River Canyon, is also of the Yosemite type, most pronouncedly so in its upper portion, which has a broad, level floor and sheer cliffs of massive granite. No cupola-shaped domes rise above its brinks, but the delicate sculpture of the Sphinx more than makes up for their absence.

In Sequoia National Park is the easily accessible Beetle Rock, a low but typical dome of exfoliating granite. Higher and more irregularly shaped, Moro Rock juts out from the mountain platform on which the Giant Forest grows, seemingly designed by nature to serve as a lookout tower commanding a vast panorama.

Of waterfalls there are many in these southern canyons, but none of great height. Rainbow Fall, on the Middle Fork of the San Joaquin, south of the Devils Postpile, makes a single beautiful leap of 150 feet over a cliff of columnar basalt, part of a volcanic flow that came from the direction of the Devils Postpile. Of interest also are the Volcanic Falls, by which Golden Trout Creek descends from its upland valley into the Kern Canyon, but these are cascades rather than leaping falls.

In depth, however, the southern canyons far exceed Yosemite Valley and even the Grand Canyon of the Tuolumne. Indeed, in the rugged drainage basins of the Kings, Kaweah, and Kern rivers mile-deep canyons are commonplace, and chasms 6,000 to 7,000 feet deep are not rare. Restricting depth measurements to flanking heights not over five miles distant, the following figures, based on topographic maps, are offered for comparison with deep canyons elsewhere.

The Upper Kern Canyon, the inner trench of which averages only 2,000 feet, at the Kern River Ranger Station attains a depth of 5,640 feet below the peaks to the west of it, and opposite Mount Kaweah it reaches a depth of 6,300 feet. The Middle Kern Canyon, throughout a stretch of twelve miles above Kernville, ranges in depth from 4,000 to more than 6,000 feet. The canyons of the South Fork, the East Fork, and the Middle Fork of the Kaweah River are all flanked by ridges and peaks 5,000 feet high, but the greatest range in altitude, nearly 7,000 feet, is found between the bed of the Middle Fork, below Redwood Meadow, and the 12,000-foot peaks of the Great Western Divide.

Deepest of all are the canyons of the Kings River and its two main forks. Above Cedar Grove, in the canyon of the South Fork, the peaks of the Monarch Divide, over 11,000 feet in altitude, stand 6,400 to 7,000 feet high. Granite Pass, the lowest gap in the Monarch Divide, rises 5,680 feet above the South Fork and 4,680 feet above Simpson Meadow, in the Middle Fork Canyon. That canyon throughout the greater part of its course maintains depths ranging from 5,500 to 6,800 feet. Below Tehipite Valley its depth increases to 7,500 feet at the junction with the South Fork. From that junction westward for a distance of five miles the main Kings Canyon is bordered on the north side by a plateau nowhere less than 7,000 feet above the river. The maximum height, at Spanish Mountain, is 8,200 feet. On the "low" south side of the canyon the upland rises more than 5,000 feet above the river.

From these figures it is evident that the Kings River Canyon is considerably deeper than the Grand Canyon of the Colorado River, which does not exceed 6,000 feet. It is deeper also than the Snake River Canyon, along the Idaho-Oregon boundary, which averages 5,500 feet. But one chasm within the limits of the United States is definitely deeper than the Kings Canyon—namely, the canyon of Lake Chelan, in the Cascade Range of north-central Washington, the bottom of which lies 8,500 to 8,650 feet below the flanking peaks. However, since the lake itself is 1,510 feet deep, the full depth of the chasm is not in view.

The Sierra Nevada is a crustal block broad enough to bear a whole system of linear mountain ranges on its back. The superimposed ranges form subordinate crests 2,000 to 5,000 feet high and dominate the landscape of the High Sierra. They also influence the arrangement of the streams on the range, for most of them trend northwestward and thus force the streams to flow either northwest or southeast instead of directly down the western slope.

Thus the Lyell Fork of the Tuolumne River flows northwest behind the Cathedral Range, and the Merced River in its upper course flows northwest behind the Clark Range. The Middle Fork of the San Joaquin is forced to flow southeast and south for a distance of fourteen miles behind the Ritter Range before it can turn westward. Even more remarkable is the South Fork of the San Joaquin, which flows northwest, behind Kaiser Ridge, for more than forty miles.

How did these northwest-trending crests on the Sierra block originate? To find the answer we must go far back in the geological history of the Sierra region—much farther back than was necessary in tracing the evolution of the Sierra itself. It will be recalled that the growth of that range was initiated by gradual uplift of a coastal lowland, shortly after the beginning of the Cenozoic period, nearly 60,000,000 years ago. (See the table of geologic time divisions, p. 64.) Some 70,000,000 years earlier, in the latter half of the Jurassic period of the Mesozoic era (the era of giant reptiles), there stood in the same place another mountain range, or, rather, mountain system, that doubtless also had great height. There is trustworthy evidence that it had been preceded by a still earlier mountain system, for mountains are short-lived, considering the total length of earth history, which is close to two billion years.

The mountain system of Jurassic time, "the ancestral sierras," like its predecessor was gradually worn down, during the long Cretaceous period, until there remained only rows of hills in a coastal lowland. Although the ancient mountains were thus almost wiped out, their "roots" remain in part preserved, incorporated in the Sierra block; from their structure we can infer the manner in which those mountains were formed and even reconstruct in imagination their topographic forms. They were not block ranges but essentially wrinkles in the earth's crust produced by the folding and crumpling of a great series of strata that originally had been laid down as flat beds on the bottom of a shallow sea. The upturned beds of slate, sandstone, and limestone in the foot-hill belt of the Sierra Nevada tell the story. Beneath those folded strata the granite welled up as a molten mass. The folds extended in a prevailingly northwestern direction, roughly parallel to one another, and so it is evident that this ancient mountain system was in many respects similar to that of the Appalachian Mountains. (See figs. 1 and 2.)

In a mountain system of that kind, the ridges are composed of the more resistant rocks, and the valleys are carved along belts of relatively weak rocks. The rivers of the ancestral sierras must have flowed parallel to the ridges, either northwest or southeast. As the Sierra region was raised to greater and greater height, these streams trenched deeper and deeper, and finally cut through the entire thickness of folded strata and into the granite underneath. So these streams as well as the ridges between them became essentially fixed in position.

As the western slope became steeper, there developed a new set of master streams flowing southwest, more or less directly down that slope. Through the gaps in the northwest-trending crests they extended headward and captured the streams of the old system; but many of the latter, unable to shift, maintained their former courses. Thus many tributaries of the present master streams, and in places even the master streams themselves, flow northwest or southeast, regardless of the southwestward slant of the Sierra block.

The secondary crests of the Sierra Nevada have inherited their northwestward trend from the ridges, or at least the structure, of the ancestral sierras. Many of them are, in fact, composed entirely of folded strata remaining from vanished mountains; others consist largely of granite but are still capped by masses of dark-hued rocks, remnants of the roof that once covered all the granite; still others are composed of granite all the way to the top.

Along the crest of the range are extensive remnants of the ancient roof rocks—sedimentary and volcanic rocks, baked and metamorphosed out of semblance to their former state. Mount Dana, Mount Gibbs, Parker Peak, and Blacktop Peak consist of such materials, as their somber but variegated hues proclaim from afar; and almost the entire eastern flank of the range is made up of these characteristically folded and twisted strata. Banner Peak, Mount Ritter, and the Minarets consist of dark-hued volcanic rocks that hung down in the molten granite, in the form of a huge roof pendant, to a depth of more than a mile. The LeConte Divide, Goddard Canyon, and Emerald Peak are carved from another large roof pendant, and many similar remnants of the ancestral sierras occur elsewhere in the High Sierra.[5]

Many crests and even some of the highest peaks consist entirely of granite: Mount Darwin, Mount Tyndall, Mount Whitney, and Mount Langley. The broad tabular summits of these peaks, indeed, may be among the oldest features in the landscape of the Sierra Nevada, for their gently sloping forms could not have been produced at high altitudes. They are survivals of a subdued topography dating from the time when the Sierra region was a lowland.[6]

The story of the titanic dislocations of the earth's crust whereby the great eastern escarpment was produced could not have been told without mention of the ancient glaciers, for it was during the Ice Age that those epochal events took place. Neither was it possible to ignore the role which the glaciers have played in the excavation and remodeling of the canyons. But there is still need of a comprehensive picture of the Sierra's glacial mantle as a whole.

The great naturalist John Muir was the first to trace the pathways of some of the ancient glaciers in the Sierra Nevada; he was increasingly impressed with their vast extent and the profound changes which they appeared to have wrought in the landscape. He became, indeed, more intimately familiar with the facts and more nearly right in their interpretation than any professional geologist of his time.

[5] Visitors to Yosemite may see these ancient rocks on their approach to the valley as they pass through the foothills, where the more resistant slates crop out like gravestones above the sod; these are termed "Mariposa slates" among geologists and are familiarly known as "gravestone slates." In and about the Yosemite itself, only a few isolated fragments of sedimentary rocks remain. On the trail to Sentinel Dome, about halfway up from Glacier Point, is a body of dark schist a hundred feet long, and at several places along the Four-mile Trail from Glacier Point to the valley are small slabs. A mass of quartzite occurs in the basin of Indian Creek and another at the northern base of Mount Clark. Beds of limestone, greatly altered (metamorphosed) by the heat of the molten granite, are found on the borders of Lake May, south of Mount Hoffmann, and in the basin of Yosemite Creek north of that mountain.

[6] See François Matthes, "The Geologic History of Mount Whitney," Sierra Club Bulletin, Vol. XXII, No. 1 (February, 1937), pp. 1–18.

But glacial geology was then in its infancy; and it has since advanced
by rapid strides. It is now known that the Sierra Nevada and the Cascade
Range, like the other higher ranges and mountain groups in the western
United States, were not overridden by the great continental glaciers of
the Ice Age but were separate centers of glaciation, and that they bore
ice chiefly in the form of mountain glaciers.

The Cascade Range to the north of the Columbia's gorge was heavily
mantled with ice, but south of the gorge, throughout Oregon and northern California, it was bare of ice, except for clusters of glaciers on the
major peaks. The twofold reason for this paucity of ice was that the range
lacked sufficient height and lay behind high coastal mountains that inter-
cepted a large proportion of the moisture brought by the westerly winds.
The Sierra Nevada, on the contrary, had the double advantage of great
altitude and of being situated to leeward of relatively low coast ranges
that let most of the moisture blowing in from the Pacific pass over them.
And so the Sierra Nevada, in spite of its southerly position and the heat
of flanking desert plains, became a great independent center of ice accumulation—the greatest in North America in that general latitude.

In Muir's day the Great Ice Age, as Agassiz called it, was conceived of
as a single prolonged and unbroken reign of snow and ice; but since
then intensive studies of the earthy and bouldery material—the glacial
drift—which the ice plastered over the lowlands of Europe and North
America have disclosed that there are four distinct layers differing markedly in degree of preservation and indicating four successive glaciations
separated by long intervals of normal climatic conditions. Thus an entirely new perspective on the history of glaciation was obtained. Moreover, it is now possible to estimate the duration of the alternating glacial
and interglacial stages which made up the Ice Age. Their total length
is probably close to a million years.

Glacial geology is now founded on the recognition of these four glacial
stages; in modern glaciological surveys in the Sierra Nevada the endeavor
has been to differentiate between the records, contained chiefly in the
moraines, of these successive glaciations. Three are found to be definitely
indicated (see pp. 47, 48), and in a few places there appears to be dim,
or only circumstantial, evidence of the fourth and earliest one.

At its extreme northern end, where the crest line averages only 7,000
feet in altitude, the Sierra Nevada was, like the Cascade Range north
of it, too low to be broadly mantled with ice. Only cirque glaciers existed
on the cool northerly flanks of the higher mountains. But fifty miles
farther south, in the vicinity of Donner Pass, where the main peaks rise
to altitudes of 8,000 and 9,000 feet, the glaciers of the latest stage attained
lengths of ten to fifteen miles and coalesced to form a continuous ice

mantle two hundred fifty square miles in extent. During the earlier stages the glaciers must have been much larger. Donner Pass itself, 7,000 feet in altitude, was during each glacial stage completely submerged beneath a great ice sea, and long glaciers descended from it both westward and eastward.

Another fifty miles farther south, where the main divide west of Lake Tahoe bears peaks 9,000 to 10,000 feet high, the later glaciers on the western slope were twenty miles long and the earlier glaciers were five to ten miles longer. East of the divide a row of cascading ice streams plunged into the basin of Lake Tahoe. And in the hundred-mile stretch from Lake Tahoe to Yosemite National Park, in which the summit peaks rise progressively to altitudes of 11,000, 12,000, and 13,000 feet and the range attains a climax of ruggedness, there developed also a grand climax of glaciation. So heavy was the snowfall there—due east of the Golden Gate, which allowed the fogs from the Pacific to penetrate inland unhindered—that a true ice cap was formed. Above its broadly domed surface only a few of the highest peaks projected as small dark "islands" of rock, *nunataks*. Along the axis of the range this ice cap extended for eighty miles; in breadth it averaged forty miles; and from its margins long, tapering ice streams reached down the canyons in both the western slope and the eastern escarpment.

Among those ice streams were the longest in the entire Sierra Nevada. In the canyons of the forks of the Stanislaus River they attained lengths of thirty miles during the latest glacial stage and of forty to forty-five miles during the earlier ages. Longest of all was the Tuolumne Glacier, which each time completely overwhelmed Hetch Hetchy Valley. During the latest glaciation it reached a length of forty-six miles, and during the earlier stages a maximum length of sixty miles. Even so, it did not extend to the foothills, but ended a full thirty miles above them. The other trunk glaciers, being shorter, ended correspondingly farther from the foothills.

The crown of the ice cap, it is worth noting, lay not directly over the crest line of the range, but several miles west of it. Yet, as is unmistakably indicated by the grooves and striae on rock floors and ledges, the pressure of the ice dome on its plastic basal layers forced part of the ice to flow uphill and eastward through the gaps in the divide.

Of the ice streams that flowed down the eastern escarpment many spread out on the adjoining lowlands. Six of them advanced into Mono Basin, and several of these reached Mono Lake, which during glacial times was 600 feet deeper and, of course, much larger than it now is. These glaciers broke off in icebergs, which carried rocks derived from the Sierra Nevada and dropped them into the lake as the ice melted.

So it happens that rock fragments from the Sierra lie strewn about on Paoha Island, which at the highest stage of the lake lay submerged to a depth of 500 feet.

The Yosemite Glacier, the next ice stream to the south of the great Tuolumne Glacier, was by far the smallest trunk glacier in the central Sierra Nevada, for it headed in a separate and relatively small basin and received only moderate reinforcements by overflow from the neighboring ice cap. During the latest stage the Yosemite Glacier attained a length of only twenty-four miles and terminated in Yosemite Valley, just below Bridalveil Fall; but during the earlier ice ages it continued down the Merced Canyon a short distance below El Portal, thus reaching a length of thirty-six or thirty-seven miles.

Southeast of the Yosemite region, in the broad drainage basin of the San Joaquin River during the earlier ice ages lay another vast ice mass. It measured fifty miles in length along the axis of the range and thirty to thirty-five miles in breadth. Taken together with the adjoining ice masses in the basins of Dinkey Creek and the North Fork of the Kings River, it formed a *mer de glace* 1,500 square miles in extent. Yet it was not a true ice cap, strictly speaking, for its surface was broadly concave rather than dome-shaped. It consisted of a large number of confluent glaciers that had descended from the surrounding peaks and crests, filled the canyons to overflowing, and spread over the intermediate uplands.

During the latest glaciation there was not enough ice to spread over so large a territory, and most of the glaciers lay confined in canyons. There were two great ice streams: the Middle Fork Glacier, which headed on Banner Peak and Mount Ritter, and the South Fork Glacier, which originated in Evolution Basin. The former measured thirty-three miles in length; the latter, forty-three miles. At Balloon Dome the two joined to form a trunk glacier, which attained a length of but three or four miles.

Entirely different was the situation in the drainage basin of the Kings River. Because of the tremendous depth of the Middle Fork and the South Fork canyons—5,000 to 7,000 feet—the trunk glaciers remained wholly separated and there could be no *mer de glace* spreading broadly across the Monarch Divide. But each of the two main ice streams headed in high-level valleys paralleling the crests of the range and filled with a continuous ice field twenty-four miles long; both ice streams received rows of cascading tributaries along their courses.

During the latest glaciation the Middle Fork Glacier, which passed through Tehipite Valley, attained a length of twenty-eight miles, and the South Fork Glacier, reinforced by the ice that came down Bubbs Creek Canyon, attained a length of thirty miles. Yet these two trunk glaciers fell short by several miles of reaching the junction of the canyons and remained wholly separate. Whether their more voluminous predecessors of the earlier ice ages effected a conjunction is a question that, to the best of the writer's knowledge, is still unanswered.

Striking indeed must have been the appearance of the Kaweah Basin during glacial times, for each of its numerous converging canyons was the pathway of a turbulent, cascading ice stream. A dozen such ice streams, five to seven miles long, descended from the Great Western Divide, yet the largest single ice mass lay in the now clean-swept basin of exfoliating granite that extends from Tokopah Valley to the tableland at the head of the Marble Fork. This ice mass covered an area of about fifteen square miles and sent forth a trunk glacier ten miles long. These figures are for the later ice streams; the extent of the earlier ones is unknown and may never be known exactly, as the older moraines are concealed by dense chaparral on the lower slopes of the canyons.

The southernmost trunk glacier in the Sierra Nevada lay in the Kern Canyon. As that canyon extends in a nearly straight line through the middle of the Upper Kern Basin, and the tributary canyons branch from it like the ribs in an oak leaf from the main rib, the glacier system had the same pattern. During the latest glaciation the tributary ice streams coming down from the Great Western Divide on the west and the main Sierra crest on the east lay confined in the side canyons; but during the earlier glaciations there was more ice than the canyons could hold and it spread over the benchlands on either side of the main canyon to a total breadth of four to six miles, thus producing a *mer de glace* about thirty square miles in extent—a truly remarkable fact, considering that the entire expanse sloped southward and lay exposed to the rays of the midday sun.

It has long been assumed that the Kern Glacier never extended beyond the terminal moraine that loops across the floor of the Kern Canyon a mile south of Golden Trout Creek. (On that curving ridge stand the boundary posts of Sequoia National Park.) However, recent investigations have shown that this moraine marks only the limits which the glacier reached during the latest ice age. During the earlier stages the glacier extended seven miles farther down the canyon to the vicinity of Hockett Peak, as is indicated by its right lateral moraines. It appears that during the latest ice age the Kern Glacier attained a length of twenty-five miles, and during the preceding ice ages a length of about thirty-two miles. Hockett Peak marks approximately the southernmost limit of glaciation in the Sierra Nevada. Farther south the range was too low to bear glaciers. Its great glacier system, three hundred miles long, thus ended abruptly just beyond the southern limit of the High Sierra.

What of the numerous existing glaciers, including those so small as

CHRONOLOGICAL SUMMARY OF THE GEOLOGIC HISTORY OF THE SIERRA NEVADA
AND TABLE OF GEOLOGIC TIME DIVISIONS

Era	Period	Epoch	Events	Duration in years
Cenozoic	Quaternary	Postglacial or Recent	2. New cirque glaciers come into existence during "little ice age"—roughly, during last 3,000 to 4,000 years. 1. Glaciers of last ice age vanish as temperatures mount above present level during "climatic optimum."	9,000
		Pleistocene (Great Ice Age)	3. Beginning after first ice age, strong faulting movements take place at intervals along eastern flank of Sierra Nevada. Country to the east sinks, the great escarpment is formed, and range remains standing as a slanting block. 2. Valleys in western slope are deepened to canyons, partly by rivers and partly by glaciers. 1. Four successive ice ages ensue; range extensively covered by glaciers.	1,000,000
	Tertiary	Pliocene	2. Final and greatest uplift at end of this epoch and beginning of next; Sierra Nevada attains substantially its present height. 1. Uplifts are followed by long interval of relative quiescence during which deep and fairly broad valleys are cut in western slope of range.	11,000,000
		Miocene and Oligocene	3. The Sierra is further bowed up, attaining height of several thousand feet. It stands high above the country to east; faulting takes place along some parts of its abrupt eastern flank. 2. In northern parts of range, broad floods of volcanic mud pour from fissures and craters near crest and bury valleys and intermediate divides on western slope. Only local flows in central and southern portions of range. 1. Minor uplifts at intervals; the Sierra is bowed up by degrees to a mountain barrier of moderate height.	26,000,000
		Eocene	2. Streams cut in, and hills begin to stand out again as low mountain ridges. 1. Lowland, stretching from the Pacific Coast far inland, is gradually upwarped.	20,000,000

CHRONOLOGICAL SUMMARY OF THE GEOLOGIC HISTORY OF THE SIERRA NEVADA
AND TABLE OF GEOLOGIC TIME DIVISIONS—*Continued*

Era	Period	Epoch	Events	Duration in years
Mesozoic	Cretaceous		2. The Sierra region by degrees is reduced to a lowland bearing northwest-trending rows of hills. 1. Ancestral sierras are subjected to long-continued stream erosion. Folded strata are worn away over large areas, and granite is broadly exposed, but northwest trend of ridges and valleys remains in part preserved.	69,000,000
	Jurassic		3. Vast masses of molten granite invade folded strata from below and slowly crystallize into hard rock. 2. Marine sediments, together with remnants of earlier mountain ranges, are folded and crumpled into parallel, northwest-trending ridges of Appalachian type. 1. Layers of mud and limy ooze thousands of feet thick are deposited in shallow sea covering site of Sierra Nevada and adjacent parts of California.	25,000,000
	Triassic		Marine sediments and volcanic rocks are deposited, but little is known of mountain-building events.	30,000,000
Paleozoic			Sediments accumulate in ocean basin to thicknesses of thousands of feet and are repeatedly raised and folded into mountain ranges.	328,000,000
Proterozoic			No definite data at hand.	?

to be termed "glacierets," that lie scattered along the Sierra crests? These glaciers of our own times were long assumed to be the relics of the vastly larger glaciers of the Ice Age and were regarded as lingering remnants doomed to eventual extinction. It is now realized, however, that these glaciers are actually "reborn" ice bodies only a few thousand years old. Their rebirth in historic times is a subject of great scientific significance, as well as of dramatic human interest. (See chap. 9.)

2

The Yosemite region and
its High Sierra

Deeply carved in the western flank of the Sierra Nevada, about midway between the torrid foothills and the wintry summits—literally and figuratively near the heart of California—lies Yosemite Valley. Compared with the entire Yosemite National Park,[1] which, with an area of 1,189 square miles, is almost as large as the state of Rhode Island, Yosemite Valley is indeed small, for it measures only seven miles long and one to two miles wide. It is, in fact, but a widened portion of the prevailingly narrow canyon of the Merced River, which traverses the southern half of the Park from east to west. Nor is it the only chasm of note within the Park. A dozen miles to the north and parallel to it is

---

[1] Established by the government in 1890. In reading the description of the Yosemite region given in this and subsequent chapters, the reader will do well to refer frequently to the excellent topographic map of the Park (scale two miles to the inch) published by the U. S. Geological Survey, Washington 25, D.C. It may be obtained from that office or at the Yosemite National Park Museum.

the Grand Canyon of the Tuolumne River, a prodigious gash which exceeds Yosemite Valley in length and in depth, though scarcely in scenic grandeur, and which opens into Hetch Hetchy Valley, a lesser yosemite that now holds an artificial lake, impounded by a dam at its lower end.

Broadly viewed, the canyons of the Tuolumne and the Merced rivers are two long furrows in the western flank of the Sierra Nevada—two of a great series of such furrows, all of notable depth and nearly all arranged roughly parallel to one another and at right angles to the crest line of the range. The Yosemite, therefore, is but one chasm in a land of many chasms. It is, however, by far the most strikingly modeled of all.

The Yosemite region includes that part of the drainage basin of the Merced River which extends from El Portal, the lower (west) entrance to Yosemite National Park; up to the heads of the Little Yosemite Valley and Tenaya Canyon, the two main branches of the Yosemite chasm; and laterally to the limiting divides on the bordering uplands. This region embraces an area twenty miles long, measured in the direction of the master stream, and twenty miles broad. Beyond its upper border lies the High Sierra; beyond its lower border, what may be called the lower Sierra slope.

A short distance above El Portal the winding, V-shaped Merced Canyon contracts abruptly to a sheer-walled gorge that has few turns, the Merced Gorge. This pronounced change in the character of the canyon is accompanied by a general change in the modeling of the landscape: the choppy, intricate ridge-and-gulch topography of the lower Sierra slope gives way to massive, billowy features. The reason is that the Yosemite region is carved of prevailingly massive, resistant granitic rocks, whereas the lower Sierra slope is made up largely of upturned slates and other thin-bedded, greatly altered sedimentary and volcanic rocks.

Proceeding up the Merced Gorge for a distance of eight miles, the traveler emerges suddenly into the spacious Yosemite Valley. On both sides its great cliffs reach up to forested uplands that extend, unbroken by side canyons, to the head of the valley. There, however, they are gashed by three converging branch chasms—the Little Yosemite, which is 2,000 feet deep; Illilouette Valley, on the south side, which is between 1,500 and 2,000 feet deep; and Tenaya Canyon, on the north side, which is nearly 4,000 feet deep. The floor of the Yosemite itself has an altitude of about 4,000 feet above sea level; the uplands rise from 7,000 feet at their lower margin to 8,000 feet at the valley head.

Between the three branch chasms the uplands continue, covered with dense forests of lodgepole pine and fir, but they are surmounted by isolated domes, peaks, and crests of bare granite. South of the Little Yosemite the upland is particularly well defined. It there rises gradually to an altitude of about 9,000 feet, terminating at the base of the Clark Range, the first great bulwark of the High Sierra. The upland on the north side of Yosemite Valley extends all the way to the Grand Canyon of the Tuolumne River, which is ten miles distant; that on the south side extends for a similar distance to the canyon of the South Fork of the Merced River. At the brinks of those canyons the uplands break off as sharply as they do at the brinks of the Yosemite chasm. They are therefore in the nature of elevated tablelands that stand essentially undissected in the broad spaces between the main canyons.

The two upland tracts, moreover, accord closely in height. In a broad view, especially from a point so far back from the brink of the Yosemite that the chasm is not visible, their billowy surfaces seem continuous and appear to be parts of one and the same westward-slanting high-level surface. This high-level surface has no local name, but, since it is a topographic feature of prime importance, which has its analogues in other parts of the Sierra Nevada, it will here be designated, so far as it lies within the limits of the Yosemite region, the Yosemite upland.

One characteristic of the Yosemite upland merits especial attention. Not one of its numerous vales and valleys that drain into the Yosemite slopes to the bottom of that chasm; on the contrary, they continue with gentle gradients to its lofty brinks and there terminate abruptly, some of them as abruptly as if cut off with a cyclopean knife. From the mouths of these "hanging valleys" leap most of the waterfalls and cascades for which the Yosemite region is renowned.

Looking down into the Yosemite from the lip of one of these hanging valleys, at a height of 2,500 or 3,000 feet, one gains the impression that the chasm is an abnormal abyss that lies sunk deep below the general level of the land. Indeed, the abrupt termination of the upland valleys at its brinks, together with the prevailing sheerness of its walls, does suggest that the Yosemite was produced by a rupturing of the earth's crust or by the caving in of a portion of it.

A typical example of a hanging valley is that of Yosemite Creek, the largest upland valley on the north side. Extending with moderate gradient to the brink, it is there cut off sharply at a height of 2,565 feet above the floor of the main chasm. From its lip pour the Yosemite Falls, the most famous of the waterfalls of the Yosemite region. The valley of Yosemite Creek is about ten miles long and traverses the entire breadth of the northern upland; one of its branches, in fact, heads close to the brink of the Grand Canyon of the Tuolumne. Much shorter is the hanging vale of Ribbon Creek, west of Yosemite Creek. This vale is cut off at a height of 3,050 feet, and from its lip descends Ribbon Fall, the highest of the Yosemite's waterfalls. On the south side, a little farther west, is the upland vale of Meadow Brook, which hangs at a height of 2,585 feet; and several miles to the east is the somewhat longer valley of Sentinel Creek, which is the highest of all, opening 3,340 feet above the Yosemite floor.

The hanging valley of Bridalveil Creek, which drains the major part of the southern upland, does not terminate abruptly at the brink but opens into a steep V-shaped gulch that projects, flanked by rocky spurs, a mile and a half into Yosemite Valley. Down this gulch, as through an immense chute, the stream glides with amazing speed, finally leaping over the 600-foot precipice at the bottom in Bridalveil Fall. Even the upland valley is not typical throughout: broad and gently sloping in its middle course, it contracts, about two miles from the brink, to a rock-walled gorge of somewhat steeper gradient. Bridalveil Creek may be said to traverse first a normal upland valley, next a somewhat steeper gorge, and then a precipitous chute, before it makes its final leap.

The hanging valleys of Indian Creek and its East Fork, which are east of Yosemite Creek, differ from any of the valleys mentioned in that their mouths are deeply gashed by V-shaped gulches, through which the streamlets cascade without making any waterfalls of note, joining each other midway in their descent. The gulch of the main stream is fully a mile long; it is known as Indian Canyon because, being unobstructed by cliffs, it served the Yosemite Indians, before the white man built his trails, as a route of egress from the valley.

Illilouette Valley is cut to much greater depth below the general level of the Yosemite upland than most of the other valleys in this group, yet it also is a true hanging valley, for it terminates abruptly 1,850 feet above the Yosemite floor. Its relatively great depth—nearly 2,000 feet—can hardly be accounted for by the volume of Illilouette Creek. That stream, it is true, is the largest of the Merced's tributaries in the Yosemite region and drains the most extensive territory of them all; but the depth of the valley seems out of proportion to the size of the stream. The same impression is created by the hanging valleys of Tamarack and Grouse creeks, in the lower part of the Yosemite region, which likewise are intermediate in height between the true upland valleys and the main chasm, yet which contain relatively small streams.

If Illilouette Valley thus seems anomalously deep, Tenaya Canyon seems vastly more so, for it is cut down within 100 feet of the level of Yosemite Valley and is, next to that valley, the greatest chasm in the Yosemite region, yet it is traversed by a streamlet comparable in volume to Yosemite Creek. Moreover, its floor lies fully 2,000 feet below that of the Little Yosemite, which is the pathway of the Merced River. However, the Little Yosemite itself seems anomalous because of its lack of depth, considering that it forms part of the canyon of the master stream. It is cut off abruptly 2,000 feet above the main Yosemite and has the aspect of a hanging valley. From its mouth the Merced descends by successive leaps, forming Nevada Fall and Vernal Fall and a chain of turbulent cascades. It will be readily understood, then, why some observers have regarded Tenaya Canyon rather than the Little Yosemite as the real upward continuation of Yosemite Valley. The paradoxical relation between the two chasms constitutes one of the most puzzling features of the Yosemite region, which is, however, fully explained by the evolutionary history of the region. (See chap. 4, p. 85.)

Both Tenaya Canyon and the Little Yosemite have hanging side valleys of the true upland type. The largest, on the north side of Tenaya Canyon, is the valley of Snow Creek, which heads on the southern slope of Mount Hoffmann. It terminates 2,500 feet above the canyon floor. On the south side of the Little Yosemite is the broadly open upland vale in which lie Starr King Meadows. The streamlet that issues from these meadows makes a precipitous descent of 1,700 feet.

The successive falls of the Merced River in its descent from the Little Yosemite form the steps of a giant stairway hewn in granite. From Glacier Point, on the south side of Yosemite Valley, this natural stairway may be viewed in its entirety, and an excellent conception may be gained of the clean-cut forms of its steps and the nature of the canyon in which it is cut. The uppermost step, from which Nevada Fall drops, is 600 feet high; the next step, which gives rise to the relatively insignificant Diamond Cascades, is about 50 feet high; the lowermost step, from which Vernal Fall drops, is more than 300 feet high. The total descent is 1,200 feet in a distance of slightly more than half a mile.

Viewed from the trail that leads directly up the giant stairway to the Little Yosemite, the steps are seen to have well-defined edges, sheer fronts, or risers, and approximately level treads. The lowermost step is the most perfectly modeled; its edge is neatly squared, and its front is vertical and straight. The tread, however, is hollowed out, like a wooden stair tread that has suffered many years of wear. In the shallow basin lies picturesque Emerald Pool. All the steps, moreover, are much broader than the stream bed. They are canyon steps, not channel steps. The river, in fact, occupies but a small part of their width. From Glacier Point it has the appearance of a mere trickle finding its way down a rugged pathway that is much too broad for its small volume. There is, nevertheless, a marked narrowing of the canyon at the edge of each step, followed by a widening on the tread below. At Vernal Fall the constriction is produced mainly by a low spur on the south side of the canyon— the spur over which the horse trail leads in laborious zigzags. At Nevada

Fall the constriction is due to two great bosses of granite, Liberty Cap and Mount Broderick, which project from the north side. Immediately behind these obstructing masses the walls again flare out abruptly to the full width of the Little Yosemite.

Stairlike steps of this type accompanied by portal-like constrictions are present also in Tenaya Canyon. There is a long series of them, extending over a distance of seven miles and making a total rise of 4,000 feet; but, with one exception, these steps are not so perfectly modeled nor are the portals accentuated as are those of the giant stairway below the Little Yosemite. Tenaya Canyon opens scarcely a hundred feet above Yosemite Valley and its floor is almost level for a distance of a mile and a half. Then it rises steeply about 500 feet, but so narrow and gorgelike is its bottom here that the effect of a step is almost lost. Yet above the rise is a relatively level, broad-floored stretch nearly a mile long that is truly suggestive of a tread.

The second step is much better defined, its front rising abruptly in the form of a cross cliff about 700 feet in height. Tenaya Creek, nevertheless, does not leap over this cliff, but issues from a narrow gorge which it has cut into the step. The southern half of the step, which is the better preserved of the two, still has a smooth, tabular top and a definite, sharp edge. The tread was originally one and a half miles long, but only its upper half remains untrenched.

The third and fourth steps are low and have short treads, but the fifth step, which is at the head of Tenaya Canyon, is remarkable both for its height and its long tread. It is one of the best-developed canyon steps in the Yosemite region. The front or riser is a sheer cliff 600 feet high that connects without break with the canyon walls on each side. Down its marvelously smooth face the waters of Tenaya Creek glide rather than drop in the form of a continuous ribbon cascade. Above this great cliff begins a relatively shallow upper canyon carved in bare granite. Its floor extends with gentle gradient for the distance of about a mile, then by a flight of minor rock steps it rises to the level of Tenaya Basin, the central feature of which is Tenaya Lake.

The High Sierra, which lies immediately above the Yosemite region, is the source of the Merced River, and from it in glacial time advanced the powerful ice streams that converged upon the Yosemite chasm. It therefore is and always has been the place of origin of the agencies that have played leading parts in fashioning the chasm.

In several respects the High Sierra differs markedly from the Yosemite region. Its sky line is formed not by the timbered swells of a rolling upland but by bare, sharp-profiled mountain crests that rise high above the timber line. The Yosemite upland, it is true, continues into the

High Sierra, but only in the form of shoulders along the sides of the main canyons. It is an inconspicuous feature beneath the majestic peaks.

The canyons in the High Sierra are less deeply cut than those in the Yosemite region. They range from less than 1,000 feet to a maximum of 2,000 feet in depth below the flanking shoulders; measured with reference to the higher peaks, however, they range from 3,000 to more than 4,000 feet in depth. Hanging valleys abound at the sides of the main canyons, but they differ from the hanging valleys of the Yosemite region in that they ascend steeply by successive stairlike steps, and they head in amphitheaters sculptured among the peaks. Lakelets of emerald and sapphire hues lie on the steps, contrasting vividly with the light buff tones of the surrounding granite. Snowbanks and snow fields fleck the mountainsides; a few small glaciers gleam in the deeper hollows.

The High Sierra is distinguished from the Yosemite region also by its vast expanses of bare rock. Not only are the peaks bare because of their great elevation, but the floors and sides of the canyons and hanging valleys are mostly bare, partly because the soil was scraped from them by the ancient glaciers, partly because the granite over large areas is sparsely fractured and affords but scant roothold for vegetation. The High Sierra as a whole, therefore, presents a singularly clean-swept appearance that would border on the desolate were it not for groves of trees, bright-green meadows, picturesque lakelets, and dazzling snow fields.

The mountain crests that traverse the High Sierra above the Yosemite region divide it into two drainage basins, those of the Merced and the Tuolumne rivers. These crests have northwestward trends, parallel to that of the main Sierra crest, and the master streams in the two basins flow northwest, approximately at right angles to the directions they pursue farther down the slope of the range.

The first mountain crest above the Yosemite region is the boldly sculptured Clark Range, which terminates in Mount Clark (11,506 feet), on the south side of the Merced. It separates Illilouette Basin and the upland south of the Little Yosemite from the Merced Basin. About eight miles farther northeast, between the Merced Basin and the Tuolumne Basin, stands the still bolder Cathedral Range, which extends from Mount Lyell (13,090 feet), the highest summit in the central part of the Sierra Nevada, northwestward to Cathedral Peak (10,933 feet). The northeast wall of the Tuolumne Basin is formed by the main crest of the Sierra Nevada, which is surmounted by Mount Dana (13,050 feet) and a long row of other peaks, between 12,000 and 13,000 feet in altitude, overlooking Mono Lake and the deserts at the eastern base of the range.

The central feature of the Merced Basin is the upper Merced Canyon, a trench about 2,000 feet deep and half a mile wide. Though narrower and less deep, parts of this canyon resemble Yosemite Valley in their modeling. Indeed, the canyon may be said to contain a succession of minor yosemites separated by more or less accentuated constrictions. The stretches which contain Merced Lake and Washburn Lake have especially pronounced Yosemite characteristics: they are broadly U-shaped, steep-sided troughs with smooth, parallel walls devoid of spurs.

The Merced Canyon rises headward by successive steps, like the canyons in the Yosemite region. Most of the steps, it is true, are low and ill defined, so that the river makes no leaping falls but only cascades, yet the essentially stairwise mode of ascent of the canyon is manifest from a longitudinal profile. Like Yosemite Valley, the upper Merced Canyon has fairly definite brinks. Its walls rise sheer to the edges of shoulders that slope at moderate angles up to the bases of the surrounding mountain crests. These shoulders, which are the equivalent of the Yosemite upland, extend, interrupted by spurs and hanging valleys, to the very head of the Merced Basin.

The hanging valleys on the side of the Clark Range are the best developed. Most of them terminate at heights of 500 to 700 feet above the floor of the main canyon, but one, Clark Canyon, terminates at a height of 2,500 feet. At the upper end of the basin several typical hanging valleys converge toward the cliff-encircled canyon head, their waters pouring down from all sides in falls and cascades. The stairwise-ascending rock floors of these hanging valleys are largely bare and in many places gleam with glacier polish. They are, indeed, the pathways of ancient glaciers and were shaped by those glaciers rather than by the present streams. The same is true of the broad rock floor of the main canyon, which for long stretches, especially below Merced Lake, is bare and highly polished.

The side valleys that head on the Cathedral Range are longer and deeper than those on the Clark Range and are flanked by mountainous spurs. In spite of their ruggedness, however, some of the high-level valleys contain attractive stretches of meadowland. Two of them, the valleys of the Maclure Fork and Echo Creek, are so deeply cut at their mouths that they have lost the aspect of true hanging valleys. Nearly all of them head in amphitheaters deeply sculptured in the body of the range, but two head in broad gaps or passes that afford easy routes of communication to the Tuolumne Basin. The valley of the Cathedral Fork of Echo Creek heads at Cathedral Pass; the valley of the twin streams Emeric Creek and Fletcher Creek heads at Tuolumne Pass.

Forming part of the region tributary to the Merced River, yet a unit distinct from the Merced Basin, Tenaya Basin, which lies above Tenaya Canyon, contains the headwaters of Tenaya Creek. It is much smaller than the Merced Basin, being only five miles long and four miles wide, and it does not head at the main crest of the Sierra Nevada, yet it is an area of peculiar interest because it was formerly the thoroughfare for large masses of glacier ice that were diverted into it from the adjoining Tuolumne Basin and went to fill Tenaya Canyon.

Tenaya Basin lies wholly above 8,000 feet—4,000 feet higher than the Yosemite Valley. Tenaya Lake lies in its center, at an altitude of 8,141 feet. On the east the basin is walled in by the sheer cliffs of Sunrise Mountain and Tenaya Peak; on the west it is flanked by the less abrupt cliffs of Mount Hoffmann and Tuolumne Peak. At its head the basin is separated from the Tuolumne Basin by a low, inconspicuous divide.

The basin as a whole is a land of bare, glistening granite. Only at the head of Tenaya Lake and for some distance below it are there stretches of verdant meadowland. The low, wavelike swells and ridges, as well as the intermediate troughs in its floor, are essentially devoid of soil and are made of smooth, sparsely fractured rock on which trees grow far apart or are absent. The rock floor and surrounding cliffs retain in many places the high polish that was imparted to them by the grinding glaciers. It was this fact that led the Indians to call Tenaya Creek Py-we-ack ("the stream of the glistening rocks").

The Tuolumne Basin is only a small part of the vast area of mountain country drained by the Tuolumne River; it is, strictly, the basin of the main branch of the river the headwaters of which are on Mount Lyell and Mount Dana. Its natural lower limit is at Tuolumne Peak and the head of the Tuolumne Canyon. Its central feature is Tuolumne Meadows, the largest of the many subalpine gardens of the High Sierra, justly famed as one of the most attractive parts of Yosemite National Park.

The basin measures roughly fifteen miles in length and ten miles in greatest breadth and has an area comparable to that of the Merced Basin. It is, however, much less rugged. The broad meadows that stretch for many miles along the river and its two principal forks take the place of a central rock-floored canyon. Because it is less deeply trenched, the Tuolumne Basin also is considerably higher than the Merced Basin. Its central meadows have an altitude of more than 8,500 feet; they lie 1,500 feet above Merced Lake and 4,500 feet above Yosemite Valley. As the meadows extend with gentle slopes to Tioga Pass and Mono Pass on the Sierra Nevada, the Tuolumne Basin affords a particularly easy route of travel across the range. The Indians quickly perceived this fact and laid their trail from Mono Lake to the Yosemite region—the historic Mono Trail—through the length of the basin. The Tioga Road, which was built in 1882–1883 to a mining camp near the main crest of the range, was laid through the Tuolumne Basin. Since this road was acquired by the government and improved for automobile traffic, Tuolumne Meadows have become the great thoroughfare for tourist travel between the Yosemite and Mono Lake.

Although the Tuolumne Basin differs markedly in configuration from the Merced Basin, the two basins have several features in common. The broad central valley of the Tuolumne, like the upper Merced Canyon, is flanked by elevated benches that are continuations of the Yosemite upland; most of the valleys on these benches are of the hanging type, opening at heights of 500 to 1,200 feet above the grassy floor. Nor do the spurs between these hanging valleys project beyond the edges of the benches; they belong wholly to the upper story of the landscape, the broad valleys of the lower story being distinctly of the smooth-sided trough type.

The benches are best developed on the south side of the basin, where they attain a breadth of several miles. Especially is this true north and northeast of Tuolumne Pass, where they form a fairly continuous, undulating platform. This high-level surface rises gradually eastward, from 9,200 feet at the base of Cathedral Peak to 10,500 feet at the base of Mount Lyell, changing in aspect from a densely wooded to a desolate and barren country.

Of peculiar interest to the sightseer as well as to the geologist are the small glaciers and ice fields that cling to the higher peaks about the Tuolumne Basin, for they represent, on a diminutive scale, the extensive ice masses that filled the basin during the Ice Age. These small ice bodies lie in well-shaded amphitheaters or on slopes with northern exposure. The Dana Glacier occupies a deep amphitheater north of the summit of Mount Dana. A somewhat broader ice mass clings to the slope north of Parker Pass. Largest and most prominent in the landscape are the glaciers on Mount Lyell and Mount Maclure. Each measures about half a mile in length, and the Lyell Glacier is fully twice as broad. Situated close together, these dazzling ice bodies combine to give this group of peaks an alpine aspect of unexcelled beauty.

The ice bodies of this area were among the first in the Sierra Nevada to be recognized as true glaciers, and because of their accessibility they have, through many years, been systematically photographed, measured, and carefully studied by the naturalist staff of Yosemite National Park. Thus there has been assembled a large body of data of almost unique value, in this country, because of their continuity and precise, quantitative character. These observations have contributed in no small measure to the interesting conclusions on the history of the glaciers of our times.

3   Yosemite Valley

"The Incomparable Valley" the Yosemite[1] is
called by those who admire and love it. Whatever the approach—whether
directly from the Great Valley of California, by the water-level highway
along the roaring Merced River; or by sudden descent from the bordering uplands, either down the dizzy zigzags of the old Big Oak Flat Road,
or over the Wawona Road which passes through a tunnel three-quarters
of a mile long and then, as one emerges into the sunlight, in one breath-
taking view discloses the entire Yosemite panorama—having once entered
the valley one is no longer left in doubt as to the reason for its fame.
For no other valley is so remarkably fashioned; and no other valley holds
within so small a compass so astounding a wealth of distinctive features.

---

[1] "Yosemite" comes from *üzümati* or *ühümati*, which in the language of the Southern
Miwoks meant "grizzly bear." It is said to have been originally the name of the tribe of
Indians who inhabited the valley, or at least of that part of the tribe which lived on the
north side of the river. The name was given to the valley, at the suggestion of Dr. Lafayette
Houghton Bunnell, by the Mariposa Battalion, the first party of white men to enter the
valley, in 1851.

Yosemite Valley is a broad, rock-hewn trough, seven miles long and one to two miles wide.[2] It is a widened part of the canyon of the Merced River, with parallel sides that are boldly sculptured and hung with waterfalls. The level floor lies 4,000 feet above the sea, and the uplands on either side rise 3,000 to 4,000 feet higher.

The valley is situated in the forest belt of the Sierra Nevada, but, owing to the fact that the cliffs on the north side are daily heated by the sun whereas those on the south side remain mostly shaded and cool, it is a meeting place for many different species representing a considerable diversity of habitats, from the chaparral of the foothill belt to the magnificent conifers of the forested uplands.

From most other parts of the Merced Canyon, and indeed from most other canyons in the Sierra Nevada, the Yosemite is distinguished by its great width relative to its depth, by its exceptionally sheer walls, and by its level, almost gradeless, floor. It is broadly U-shaped in cross section. Even in the portal between El Capitan and the Cathedral Rocks, which is the narrowest part of the valley, the floor is many times broader than the channel of the river. By contrast, the canyon immediately above and immediately below the valley is little more than a narrow, V-shaped gorge. In the valley, moreover, the river has so gentle a gradient that it meanders in leisurely fashion, but in the gorges above and below it makes a direct, tumultuous descent. The absence of prominent spurs gives the valley an open aspect and permits a vista to be had from one end almost through to the other, in spite of the fact that its course is sinuous. Muir aptly likened the Yosemite to "an immense hall or temple lighted from above."

In depth the valley does not greatly exceed the deepest of the other parts of the Merced Canyon; it measures between 3,000 and 4,000 feet. But in the valley the effect of depth is enhanced, in spite of the breadth of the floor, by the boldness of the cliffs, the continuity of the bordering plateau-like uplands, and the seeming deliberateness with which the great waterfalls descend from the lofty rims.

Because of its walled-in character, its sequestered position more than halfway up the flank of the Sierra Nevada, and the ruggedness of the surrounding country, the Yosemite was originally very difficult to reach. The Merced Canyon in its primeval wildness afforded no convenient approach. The early routes of travel to the Yosemite were only precarious trails for pack animals over the mountainous uplands. The horse-

---

[2] Most of the features of Yosemite Valley referred to in this and succeeding chapters are indicated on the topographic map of Yosemite National Park. A much better guide for the valley itself, however, is the large-scale topographic map of Yosemite Valley, which shows it on a scale of 2,000 feet to the inch, permitting great detail and a high degree of accuracy. This map, which was surveyed by François Matthes, is published by the United States Geological Survey.

back journey was an arduous one that took several days. The traveler was obliged to ascend laboriously to altitudes of 5,000 and 6,000 feet and then descend 1,000 to 2,000 feet to reach the floor of the valley. A vivid portrayal of these old-time conditions was given by Professor Joseph LeConte in his delightful narrative of his first excursion to the High Sierra in 1870.[3]

In the 'fifties and 'sixties of the last century, wagon roads were extended from the foothills to mining camps west and south of the Yosemite, but it was not until 1874 that roads were opened to the valley itself (the Coulterville and Big Oak Flat roads). The picturesque four-horse stage then made its appearance and, although the roads were steep, rough, and dusty, tourist travel increased rapidly. The completion of the Yosemite Valley Railroad in 1907 afforded a much easier approach; it continued to serve until 1937, when, after several miles of track in the Merced Canyon were washed out during a spring flood, it was abandoned. The first motor stage entered the valley in 1913. By 1916 travel by motor car was rendered possible also in an eastward direction by the improvement of the old wagon trail known as the Tioga Road. Thus a scenic route was opened to the crest of the Sierra and then by another road to Mono Lake.

The construction of the state highway up the Merced Canyon, to connect with the government road at El Portal, may be regarded as the crowning achievement in man's conquest of the mountain wilderness that guards the Yosemite. This highway, a well-graded, all-year route, is now the main artery of Yosemite-bound traffic. However, the Big Oak Flat Road and the spectacular Wawona Road, which is kept open during the winter except for short periods after unusually heavy snows, are popular approaches to the valley, and are chosen by many because they provide opportunities to visit groves of Big Trees (*Sequoia gigantea*).

The sequestered position of the valley accounts also for the lateness of its discovery by white men. To the Spanish settlers in California the chasm remained unknown. The great mountain range which from afar they named Sierra Nevada was a forbidden land of mystery and lurking enemies. Even the early American miners who dug for gold in the foothills were unaware of the existence of the Yosemite Valley for two years, although it was only thirty or forty miles away.

The valley was probably first viewed from a distance by Joseph Reddeford Walker, who in 1833 crossed the Sierra Nevada by Mono Pass and, guided by Indians, made his way westward over the upland north of the valley. But the effective discovery of the Yosemite, through which it

---

[3] Joseph LeConte, *A Journal of Ramblings through the High Sierra of California* (San Francisco, 1875); republished in *Sierra Club Bulletin*, Vol. III (1900), pp. 1–107; republished in book form (ed. by Francis P. Farquhar) by the Sierra Club in 1930.

became known to the world, was not made until March, 1851, when the Mariposa Battalion of volunteers under Major James D. Savage, in pursuit of Chief Ten-ei-ya (Tenaya) and his marauding band of Yosemite Indians, unexpectedly came upon the natural stronghold of the tribe after a hard march over the snow-covered mountains.

Extraordinary though it may be, the Yosemite Valley is not unique. The Sierra Nevada contains several other valleys of essentially the same type. In the upper Merced Canyon, about two miles above the Yosemite and at a level 2,000 feet higher, is the Little Yosemite. Hetch Hetchy Valley, at the lower end of the Grand Canyon of the Tuolumne, though only half as long and half as wide, bears a striking resemblance to the Yosemite, having the same proportions of depth to width and the same type of cliff sculpture. Muir, who loved to dwell in the Hetch Hetchy, sometimes referred to it as the "Tuolumne Yosemite."

In the canyon of the Middle Fork of the Kings River, about eighty miles southeast of the Yosemite, is the famed Tehipite Valley, which, though only one and a half miles long and three-quarters of a mile wide, rivals the Yosemite in scenic grandeur. Tehipite Dome is, in fact, as strikingly modeled as any of the major rock forms in the Yosemite region. About ten miles southeast of the Tehipite is the great yosemite of the South Fork of the Kings River, popularly known as the Kings River Canyon. It is nine miles long—two miles longer than the Yosemite—but is narrower. Nor are its walls so high, so sheer, so impressively modeled as those of Yosemite Valley. The Kings River Canyon, however, is surrounded by titanic peaks that rise 5,000, 6,000, and even 8,000 feet above its floor.

While it is true that none of these other "yosemites" equals the original in diversity of rock forms or in wealth of waterfalls, their occurrence in different parts of the Sierra Nevada is highly significant and must be taken into account in any discussion of the Yosemite's origin.

One may describe the Yosemite, in brief, as a broadly U-shaped chasm having sheer, spurless walls and an almost flat floor; in detail, however, the valley is far from having the geometric simplicity of form that might be suggested by this characterization. Its sides do not consist of monotonous, blank walls. They are diversified by a host of boldly sculptured features and are adorned by waterfalls. The Yosemite, indeed, owes its unique place among the valleys of the world not only to its general form but to its wealth of monumental rock masses and the splendor and variety of its falling waters.

The cliffs of Yosemite Valley, though remarkably sheer in places, are at no point strictly vertical throughout their height. Almost everywhere the declivities are broken by slopes or ledges, and the bases of the walls

project considerably beyond the tops. By actual measurement the horizontal distance from top to base of the walls averages more than half a
mile. Even at those points where the cliffs are most sheer the horizontal
distance is considerably greater than a mere stone's throw. The cliffs
below Glacier Point, which are noted for their abruptness, rise 3,200
feet in a distance of a quarter of a mile. El Capitan, the boldest of all
the rock masses that flank the valley, rises 3,000 feet in a distance of 600
feet. Because of this lack of real verticality of its sides, the Yosemite is
less than half as wide at the bottom as it is at the top; from brink to brink
it measures two miles across, but its floor, measured from cliff base to
cliff base, is less than a mile wide. In places the talus slopes reduce it to
less than half a mile.

Yosemite Valley is divided by a marked constriction about a third of
the way from its lower end, between El Capitan and the great promontory
of which the Cathedral Rocks are the main summits. This imposing portal never fails to impress the incoming traveler with the stupendous scale
on which the Yosemite is built. El Capitan really juts out but little from
the north wall, but the Cathedral Rocks project fully a mile from the
south wall. Yosemite Valley thus consists of two broad chambers connected by a portal. The lower and smaller chamber is the less impressive
of the two, being enclosed only in part by precipitous cliffs, in part by
long and rather monotonous slopes of rock waste. These slopes nevertheless have a redeeming quality: they have enabled man to build roads
from the uplands to the valley floor—the Big Oak Flat Road on the
north side, the Wawona Road on the south. In no other part of the
Yosemite would it have been possible to construct roads making a descent
of 2,000 or 3,000 feet without tunneling through the cliffs.

The lower end of the valley is in the main spoon-shaped. It is closed
off by a slope of solid rock about 800 feet in height which is cut only
by the narrow, steep-walled gorge through which the Merced River
leaves the valley. This rock slope leads up to high rock benches that
extend along both sides of the Merced Gorge for several miles.

The upper or main chamber of Yosemite Valley is five and a half miles
long and has a sinuous course. Its sides are on the whole remarkably
equidistant and, although carved in a multitude of spectacular features,
have the appearance of being planed off parallel to each other. The
salients on one side correspond roughly to the embayments on the other
side. There is, however, considerable variation in width from point to
point. Immediately above the portal at El Capitan, which is about half
a mile wide, the width from cliff base to cliff base increases to a maximum of more than one mile. Farther up it contracts to 3,500 feet, then
to 3,000 feet, but widens to a full mile at the upper end of the valley.

Most strangely modeled is the valley head. It is squared off, at right angles to the sides, by a high, straight cliff a mile in length. At the north end of this wall is the broad U-shaped mouth of Tenaya Canyon; at the south end opens the narrow, tortuous gorge through which the Merced River descends from the Little Yosemite. Except for these two openings the head of the valley is bordered by continuous, massive cliffs which rise sheer almost from the valley floor, their bases being masked by small piles of debris. As a result the valley head has a boxed-in appearance.

Yosemite Valley owes its scenic character not merely to its great depth and unusual form, but in large measure to the distinctive sculpture of its walls. The rock forms are astonishingly varied in design—some massive, colossal, and simple in outline, others frail and intricately chiseled; some conspicuous for their boldness, others carved in bas-relief. Many are of such singularly clean-cut, monumental character that they impress themselves upon the memory of the beholder at once and forever.

El Capitan stands preëminent among the massive, bulky forms. Its great cliff—the most majestic in the Yosemite and perhaps in the world— rises from the valley with so simple a sweep of line that its height is peculiarly difficult to evaluate at a glance. The estimates of the first white men to camp at the foot of El Capitan now seem ludicrous. As Bunnell relates in his account of the discovery of the Yosemite Valley by the Mariposa Battalion, "One official estimated El Capitan at 400 feet; Captain Boling at 800 feet. . . . My estimate was a sheer perpendicularity of at least 1,500 feet." Trigonometric measurements made in the survey for the topographic map of the valley have determined the height of the cliff, from its toe to the brow at the top, to be fully 3,000 feet. The dome-shaped crown above the brow rises 500 feet higher.

Opposite El Capitan is the ponderous group of the Cathedral Rocks, which project more than a mile into the valley. The three summits, carved from a single asymmetric ridge, loom one above another in an ascending series. They stand 1,650, 2,590, and 2,680 feet, respectively, above the valley floor. On the west side they slope evenly to the gulch through which the waters of Bridalveil Creek race to the precipice of Bridalveil Fall. Parallel to them, on the opposite side of the gulch, is a lesser ridge the main summit of which is known as the Leaning Tower, because it actually leans out over the 1,200-foot precipice beneath.

In the embayment east of the Cathedral Rocks, in striking contrast, stand the two slender, tapering shafts of the Cathedral Spires, the frailest of all the rock forms in the valley. They rise to heights of 2,160 and 1,950 feet above its floor. Farther east are a multitude of finely chiseled, hackly forms, followed by a series of strongly asymmetric spurs with smooth slopes on the west side and vertical or overhanging cliffs on the east side. The spur under Taft Point is a notable example, but the asymmetric type of sculpture reaches its finest development on the opposite side of the valley, in the group of the Three Brothers, whose gabled forms rise one above another, all pitching at the same angle, as if designed by an architect.

Farther up the valley, vertical and horizontal lines of sculpture predominate. Sentinel Rock stands forth from the south wall like an obelisk with sheer front and sharp, splintered top. The great cliff over which Upper Yosemite Fall leaps is nearly vertical, and so is the rock wall west of it, which dominates the zigzag trail to the top of the fall. Below, on both sides of the recess in which Lower Yosemite Fall descends, are two horizontal rock terraces with sheer fronts.

Most impressive of all for height and verticality is the famous cliff at Glacier Point. It is a straight wall, a quarter of a mile long and 1,000 feet high, that abruptly terminates the promontory. That it is really vertical, and not merely inclined at an acute angle, like the majority of the cliffs that are popularly termed sheer or vertical, is evident from the silhouette profile. It is this absolute verticality of the rock face that permits the firefall, which customarily is produced every night during the tourist season by pushing the glowing embers of a bonfire from the edge of the platform above, to descend through space untrammeled, deploying gradually like a waterfall of the Yosemite type.

At the extreme top of the precipice, which is 3,200 feet above the valley, projects a large, rough slab—the famous overhanging rock of Glacier Point, which has become a veritable mecca for tourists by reason of its matchless view. A short distance to the west is a second smaller overhanging rock, known as Photographer's Rock.

The most remarkable rock forms cluster about the head of Yosemite Valley. Directly opposite Glacier Point are the Royal Arches, a series of immense natural arches carved in bas-relief, one within another, in a slanting rock face 1,500 feet high. Flanking them, as a corner post, at the mouth of Tenaya Canyon stands the Washington Column, a colossal pillar 1,700 feet in height; surmounting them is North Dome, a smoothly rounded, helmet-shaped mass of bare granite that rises 3,530 feet above the valley. A short distance to the northeast is Basket Dome, a less symmetrical dome of the same type.

Dome-shaped features of bare granite abound in the upper Yosemite region. Most readily accessible to the sightseer is Sentinel Dome, which stands on the upland, southwest of Glacier Point. Highest of all, and least accessible, is Mount Starr King, the beautifully symmetrical, egg-shaped dome east of Illilouette Valley. It is surrounded by several less conspicuous domes that seem almost insignificant in comparison with it, though each of them is actually larger than Sentinel Dome. To the general category of domes belong also Mount Broderick and Liberty Cap, the two bosses of granite that obstruct the mouth of the Little Yosemite; Cascade Cliffs, Bunnell Point, Moraine Dome, and Sugar Loaf, near the head of that valley; and the rounded back of Mount Watkins, which is really a second El Capitan that rises sheer 3,000 feet above Tenaya Canyon.

The most colossal, strangely modeled rock monument in the Sierra Nevada is Half Dome, which, planted as on a pedestal, stands at the head of Yosemite Valley, on the divide between Tenaya Canyon and the Little Yosemite. Rounded on the south side and cut off sheer on the north side, it has the appearance of a great dome which has been split in two and whose other half has been destroyed. Measured from southwest to northeast, parallel to its sheer front, it is nearly a mile long; measured at right angles to the front it is a quarter of a mile broad; from the base of the cliff to the extreme summit it is 2,200 feet high. The base of the cliff, however, is itself 2,570 feet above the level of Mirror Lake; hence the total height of the dome above Tenaya Canyon is 4,770 feet. Though formerly inaccessible, Half Dome may now be scaled with the aid of steel cables which serve as handrails.

Only one eminence in the Yosemite region outtops Half Dome—namely, the lofty ridge that culminates in Clouds Rest, at an altitude of 9,929 feet. It faces Tenaya Canyon with a cliff front two miles long and almost a mile high—one of the greatest continuous fronts of bare granite in the Sierra Nevada. The rock face is not, however, as sheer as that of El Capitan, but slants at an angle and is diversified by billowy salients and smoothly concave hollows. Beyond Clouds Rest spreads the vast panorama of the High Sierra, its jagged peaks culminating in Mount Lyell.

Every one of the rock forms enumerated is of a distinctive character, wholly different from the rock features commonly found in canyons and mountain valleys. Even in the other yosemites of the Sierra Nevada, which are carved in granitic rocks of the same general type, such exceptional forms occur isolated or in small groups. The Hetch Hetchy has its Kolana, the Tehipite its towering dome, the Kings River Canyon its Grand Sentinel and Sphinx, but none can match the Yosemite's wealth of sculpture.

4 Yosemite through the ages

Though Yosemite Valley seems in a class by itself, created in some special, unusual way, the Sierra Nevada contains other valleys of essentially the same type, other "yosemites," they have been called, which differ from the Yosemite in degree rather than in kind. So great is the similarity of these valleys that one cannot escape the conclusion that they have had a similar genesis, and were formed as a result of geologic changes which affected the Sierra Nevada as a whole.

Some 60,000,000 years ago the Sierra region was a coastal lowland with a warm, humid climate that supported lush vegetation. Early in the Tertiary period began the successive uplifts by which the Sierra Nevada eventually came into existence, and warpings bowed up the range into an asymmetric arch of increasing height. At first the Sierra block had only moderate altitude and a gentle westward slant, but in late Tertiary time it was raised, together with the country to the east, several thousand feet higher, and its slant was correspondingly steepened. At the end of

Tertiary and the beginning of Quaternary time it was still more strongly tilted, and its eastern edge was lifted to its present great height. Early in the Ice Age, when the Owens Valley and the other basins to the east sank down, the range came to stand out as it does today, with an abrupt eastern front and a long western slope.

One effect of the tilting was to rearrange the waters on the Sierra block. The main streams originally drained in diverse directions, but when the slant became sufficiently steep a new system of rivers was formed that flowed southwest, roughly parallel to one another. Thus the course of the Merced was established, and the position of Yosemite Valley was determined.

At this time along the Merced's course there was still a veneer of folded sedimentary rocks over the granite. It was not until later in its history that the river wore its channel down through the sedimentary rocks and into the granite. Then, being well entrenched and unable to deviate widely from its original course, it had to cut the jointed and the massive granitic rocks alike. The Merced is, indeed, what geologists term a "superimposed" stream, as are most of the other rivers on the western slope of the range. Therein is explained the origin of Yosemite Valley and of all the other yosemites in the Sierra Nevada. Each of the capacious U-shaped valleys has been developed in an area of prevailingly fractured rocks in which the agents of erosion worked with comparative facility and in which the glaciers, when they came upon the scene, quarried with extraordinarily great effect. The narrow portals and gorges above and below the yosemites, on the contrary, are cut in bodies of prevailingly massive rock which the glaciers could not quarry but could reduce only by slow grinding.

Canyon cutting by the rivers must have been an inevitable consequence of the uplifts of the Sierra region and the tiltings of the Sierra block; for when the slope of a stream is appreciably steepened its flow is greatly accelerated and the wear on its bed is correspondingly increased. This is what happened each time the gradients of the Merced and other Sierra rivers were steepened by an uplift of the range. With each renewed tilting, as these streams were accelerated and they more vigorously attacked their beds, they entrenched themselves in gorges which in time were enlarged into canyons or valleys, the floors of which lay at new and lower levels.

These valleys cut within valleys are tremendously significant characters, written large in the Sierra landscape, from which the trained student of mountain land forms may read—and in imagination reconstruct, on an exact, quantitative basis—the record of the successive stages by which Yosemite and its sister valleys have evolved. And, though it may sound like romance, Yosemite's great waterfalls provide some of the most critical clues to an understanding of the origin of the valley.

The successive stages in valley cutting are particularly well preserved in the unglaciated lower regions of the Sierra canyons, which give a sound basis for interpreting the development of individual canyons. Thus, in the broad view of the Lower Merced Canyon, looking westward from the summit of El Capitan, one can see that the long, even-topped ridges, declining gently toward one another, outline the broadly flaring profile of a very ancient and rather shallow valley.

Below this ancient valley appear the much better preserved features of a somewhat narrower and steeper-sided valley, evidently of less remote origin. This valley was fully 1,500 feet deep, yet it also had a broad and fairly level floor, as is shown by the numerous flats and gently undulating surfaces that remain. The Big Meadow flat, which is a few miles northeast of El Portal and is traversed by the Coulterville Road, is the principal remnant of this old valley floor in the Yosemite region.

Sharply incised in the floor of the old valley is the narrow, V-shaped inner gorge through which the Merced now flows. The gorge is 1,500 to 2,000 feet deep, but is so narrow that in the distant perspective it seems like a mere slotlike winding trench.

What is commonly and loosely termed the Merced Canyon, then, consists really of a steep-walled inner gorge cut into the floor of a spacious older valley, which in turn lies within a broad valley of still greater antiquity. Similar "three-story" profiles characterize also the lower canyons of the Tuolumne and the San Joaquin rivers; indeed, sculptural elements expressive of three stages of valley and canyon cutting may be discerned in the unglaciated lower course of every great Sierra canyon unless volcanic flows have interfered with its development. The experienced eye may recognize them even in the glaciated upper courses of some canyons, for the remodeling action of the ice has not everywhere been so thoroughgoing as to wipe out these preglacial features.

When the Merced in early Tertiary time first established its course conformably to the southwestward slant of the Sierra region, it fashioned for itself a broad, level valley of moderate depth that sloped gently seaward. Toward the headwaters of the river the land was more mountainous, but the region as a whole lay near sea level.

This first stage in the cutting of the Merced Canyon, in which it was a simple "one-story" valley (fig. 4) may be termed the broad-valley stage. For all its remoteness, it is not difficult to picture the Yosemite in that early stage, as there are abundant data from which the conditions may be restored, and in the Yosemite region the shapes of the flanking hills and ridges remain much the same. The landscape of the Yosemite region in the broad-valley stage (end of the Miocene epoch) has been carefully reconstructed in a bird's-eye view (pl. 2). This view and the others in the sequence of six which depict the evolution of the Yosemite through the ages (pls. 2–7) are all from the same assumed high point and are drawn to scale, enabling one to trace the changes stage after stage.

The Yosemite was then a broadly open, level-floored valley flanked by rolling hills and occasional ridges most of which stood 500 to 1,000 feet above the valley. Through this valley the river flowed sluggishly in broad meanders. The crown of El Capitan, which then had much the same rounded contour as now, rose in gentle curves to a height of 900 feet. Sentinel Dome stood somewhat more than 1,000 feet high, and Half Dome, a bulky, irregular mass that fell off on the northwest side in a steep, ravined slope, but not a cliff, reared its summit 1,500 feet above the valley.

The landscape was characterized by subdued, billowy forms and smooth, curving lines. Cliffs, pinnacles, and other angular forms were absent. The Cathedral Rocks were represented only by a massive, hummocky spur that sloped gradually to the valley floor. The Leaning Tower did not yet lean, but was a mere knob on another somewhat narrower spur. The Cathedral Spires and Sentinel Rock were still to be carved from the sloping south side of the valley, and the high ridge which Glacier Point surmounts was not yet cut off by a precipice, but continued northward as a projecting spur. Another still longer spur sloped from the base of Half Dome to the confluence of Tenaya Creek and the Merced River.

Fig. 4 (*facing*). Development of the Yosemite Valley (drawn to scale).

1. The "one-story" valley: The broad-valley stage of late Miocene time, when the Sierra region was still relatively low.

2. The "two-story" valley: The mountain-valley stage of late Pliocene time, a result of the first strong tilting of the Sierra block. *A–A* is the profile of a side stream which was unable to trench as rapidly as the Merced; its valley has therefore remained hanging. *B–B* is the profile of a side stream that succeeded in "catching up" with the trenching.

3. The "three-story" canyon: The canyon stage of early Quaternary time, just before the oncoming of the Ice Age—a result of the latest great uplift of the Sierra block. The river has cut its inner gorge so rapidly that now the valley of the stream *B–B* has been left hanging. But a third stream *C–C*, more favored than the others because of less resistant rock in its path, has succeeded in keeping pace with the trenching of the river.

4. The present Yosemite Valley: The transformation from the original "three-story" canyon was accomplished mainly by the quarrying action of the glaciers of the Ice Age. The floor of the glacial trough is at *D*, the present valley floor is at *E*, and *D–E* is the depth of the basin of ancient Lake Yosemite, which is now filled with river sediment. As a result of further deepening of the chasm and its widening by the ice, the valley of the stream *C–C* now also hangs, so that there are three sets of hanging valleys, one above another, all having waterfalls pouring from their mouths.

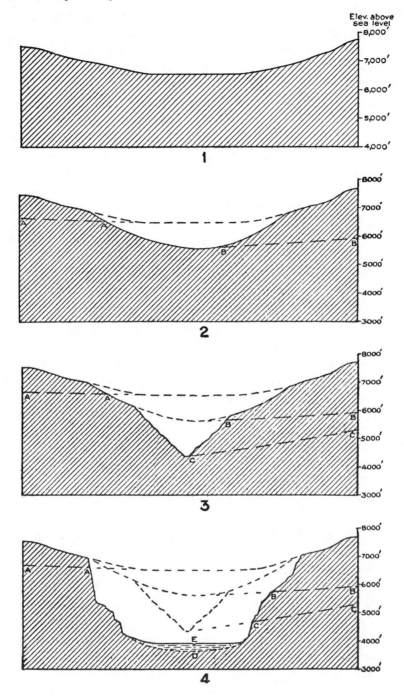

Neither were there any waterfalls or cascades in the landscape. All the tributary streams entered the main valley at the level of its floor and emptied into the placid master stream with scarcely a ripple. The giant stairway at the mouth of the Little Yosemite had not yet been hewn, and the Merced River wound lazily in serpentine curves down a gently sloping valley floor. Tenaya Creek occupied a valley commensurate in size with its small volume—a valley that lay somewhat higher than the path of the Merced and was flanked by wooded slopes. The entire region was densely covered with rain-loving vegetation—laurel, magnolia, maple, sycamore, and willow. It is probable, however, that Clouds Rest already had some cliffs of bare granite, and that Mount Starr King had much the same domed form that it has today, for massive granite produces cliffs and domes even in regions of humid climate (as is attested by Stone Mountain, Georgia, and other mountains in the southern Appalachian region).

The peaks and crest of the High Sierra stood far above the general level of the country, just as they now stand above the Yosemite upland, but they were full-bodied and rounded in contour instead of angular and hollow-sided as they now are. Their sides sloped in gentle curves to the broad floors of the Merced Basin and the Tuolumne Basin, neither of which had yet been trenched below the shoulders and benches that now flank them.

The great uplifts of late Tertiary time, which raised the Sierra block to a height of several thousand feet, affected the Merced River profoundly. Since the course of the river was steeper, its flow became swift and powerful. It abandoned its meandering habit, and with the sand, gravel, and boulders that it swept along it began vigorously to deepen its valley. In time it cut in the broad floor of its old valley a narrow, steep-walled gorge. The river cut ever more slowly as its gradient became flatter, but near the end of the Pliocene epoch it had entrenched itself almost a thousand feet. Meanwhile, the sides of the gorge were worn back to slopes of moderate inclination, and thus at length the inner gorge developed into a V-shaped inner valley of considerable depth and breadth. In the thin-bedded and relatively weak rocks of the lower slope of the Sierra Nevada, the inner valley grew to be very broad—in places so broad as to obscure the older valley in which it was cut. But higher, in the prevailingly massive and resistant granitic rocks of the Yosemite region, the inner valley remained relatively narrow and steep-sided. And so the river lay at the bottom of a valley within a valley, that is, a "two-story" valley (fig. 4).

The side streams were at first unable to trench as rapidly as the Merced. They had smaller volume and therefore less cutting power, and a number of them were handicapped by following courses that lay at right angles to the general course of the river and therefore at right angles to the slope of the Sierra block. These streams were not steepened by the tilting and continued to flow as leisurely as before. As the river cut its gorge deeper and deeper, therefore, the side valleys remained hanging at greater and greater heights. But later, as the master stream's gradient became flatter and its cutting power waned, most of the side streams by degrees "caught up" with its trenching and the hanging valleys were cut down, except for a few in the Yosemite region that were underlain by very resistant, massive granite. These remained almost untouched, and so, at the end of Tertiary time, the Yosemite was left with several hanging side valleys from whose lips poured foaming cascades.

As the inner valley maintained the aspect of a rugged mountain valley, this second stage in the cutting of the Merced Canyon may be termed the mountain-valley stage. The reconstructed landscape of the mountain-valley stage (end of Pliocene epoch) is portrayed in plate 3. It is less easy to depict than the broad-valley stage, for the valley had become much deeper and more complexly modeled. The Yosemite had developed into a broadly V-shaped and fairly rugged mountain valley about 1,600 feet deep. It was flanked by uplands, for a number of tributary valleys had not been cut down to its level. No sharp rims defined the edges of the uplands, but the change in declivity from upland surface to valley side was fairly abrupt. El Capitan had a distinct brow separating its rounded summit from the new, steep slope below. The brow rose 1,200 feet above the floor of the valley, but the drop was distributed over a horizontal distance of about half a mile, and consequently the slope was not marked by precipitous cliffs. Probably it was, like the valley sides elsewhere, largely wooded, though, owing to the massive structure of the granite, it must have been studded with crags and pinnacles.

The Cathedral Rocks formed an asymmetric spur, much steeper on the east side than on the west and surmounted by two knobs corresponding to the two higher summits of the present group. The highest of these knobs stood about 900 feet above the floor of the valley. The third and lowest summit of the present group was still to be hewn from the rock below the level of the valley floor.

The Cathedral Spires and the other crags in their neighborhood were only dimly foreshadowed by rocky spurs separated by deep ravines. In the place of Sentinel Rock was an irregular spur that projected far out into the valley and deflected the river to the north. Eagle Peak, less sharply attenuated than it is today, was the culminating summit of a massive asymmetric spur that deflected the river to the south. It stood fully 1,700 feet above the water.

Half Dome was probably a long ridge, with the northwest side, furrowed by ravines and mostly wooded, carrying no suggestion of a sheer cliff with overhanging cornice. The southeast side in all likelihood was already in part smoothly curved and bare. The crest of the ridge rose at least 2,200 feet above the Little Yosemite and about the same height above the valley of Tenaya Creek. That stream joined the Merced opposite Glacier Point, but owing to the increased depth of their valleys the tapering spur between them had assumed much greater relative height. The granite from which the Washington Column and the cliff of the Royal Arches were later carved still lay beneath the level of the valley.

The most distinctive feature of the Yosemite landscape of that early epoch was the array of cascades foaming from the mouths of the hanging upland valleys, although there were probably no leaping waterfalls. Yosemite Creek tumbled 600 feet from a hanging valley. It had carved a gulch one and three-fourths miles long, the head of which is now one mile back from the rim. Ribbon Creek had the highest hanging valley, and cascaded 1,400 feet in a horizontal distance of somewhat less than a mile. Meadow Brook made a mile-long cascade of 1,200 feet through a gulch that headed just back of the present upland rim. Bridalveil Creek descended about 900 feet through a gulch two and a half miles long, and Sentinel Creek made a much steeper cascade of 900 feet through a gulch less than a mile long that headed not as far back as the present upland rim.

Only a few tributary streams had cut their valleys to the level of the Merced and joined that river without cascades or falls. Among these were Indian Creek, Illilouette Creek, and Tenaya Creek. The basin of Indian Creek today still has the general character it acquired during the mountain-valley stage, having been changed only slightly by glaciation. Illilouette Basin has been modified more significantly by the glaciers, but for the most part only locally; thus it also retains in a broad way the configuration of the mountain-valley stage. The present appearance of Tenaya Canyon, on the contrary, gives no suggestion whatever of the mountain-valley it replaces. The depth of the valley is, however, reliably indicated by the hanging valley of Snow Creek and by the upper Tenaya Basin. That basin, indeed, may be regarded as a large remnant of the mountain-valley landscape, severely though not profoundly remodeled by the ice.

The Little Yosemite in the mountain-valley stage had been cut to a depth of about 1,200 feet. Liberty Cap, still a mere knob on a low spur that projected, uninterrupted by any gaps, southward from the base of Half Dome, stood only 600 feet above its floor. Above the Little Yosemite the mountain valley cut by the Merced extended in the form of a narrow central trench all the way to the head of the Merced Basin. It was the

antecedent of the present broad and deep glacial trough in which lie
Merced Lake and Washburn Lake, but it decreased rapidly in depth
toward its head, and thus the side valleys hung at no great height above
its floor.

At the end of the Tertiary and the beginning of the Quaternary periods came the latest and greatest uplifts and tilting movements, those
that resulted in the elevation of the Sierra Nevada to its present height.
The sources of the Merced were then raised not less than 6,000 feet
above their previous altitude. The general slope of the river was greatly
steepened; torrential waters deepened the river bed, scouring it with
sand and gravel, pounding it with boulders, and plucking out slabs and
blocks wherever the fractured state of the rock permitted. The greatly
increased height of the range brought with it a marked change in climate.
Deep snows fell on the crest in winter, and the rapid melting of the
snows in spring produced freshets of tremendous volume and destructive
power. Thus the river again entrenched itself and with greater rapidity
than before carved a new inner gorge, producing a "three-story" canyon
(fig. 4).

In this new inner gorge the river still flows from the lower end of
Yosemite Valley to the foothills. At El Portal, the main gate to Yosemite
National Park, the gorge attains its greatest depth—2,000 feet, or about
twice the depth of the Pliocene mountain valley—yet the time involved
in cutting this gorge has been probably less than a million years. That
the cutting is still in progress is shown by the fact that even in its lower
course, where it traverses relatively unresistant rocks, the river still flows
in a rock channel and makes cascades over the more obdurate ledges.

As happened after the preceding uplift, so after the last, the side
streams, especially those running at right angles to the direction of the
tilting, were unable to trench as rapidly as the master stream. And so
Yosemite Valley, which already had one set of hanging valleys, acquired
a second, lower set. To this lower set belong the valleys of Indian Creek
and Illilouette Creek. Both of them, as well as some of the hanging side
valleys of the lower Merced Canyon, are still well preserved, although
they are underlain by less resistant rocks than the older and higher hanging valleys of the region. Indeed, so short a time, in a geologic sense,
has elapsed since the last uplift that only a few of the more favorably
situated side streams have succeeded in "catching up" with the trenching
of the master stream.

Among these successful streams are two that enter the Merced in Yosemite Valley—Tenaya Creek and Bridalveil Creek. Tenaya Creek had
the double advantage of a southwesterly course, following the direction
of the tilting, and of being underlain by closely fractured rock, and was

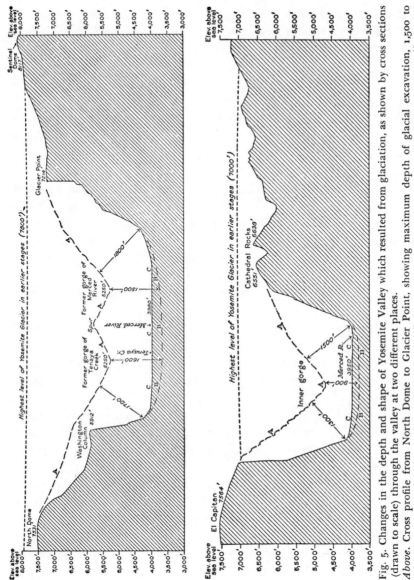

Fig. 5. Changes in the depth and shape of Yosemite Valley which resulted from glaciation, as shown by cross sections (drawn to scale) through the valley at two different places.

Above. Cross profile from North Dome to Glacier Point, showing maximum depth of glacial excavation, 1,500 to 1,600 feet. *A–A,* Preglacial profile; *B–B,* approximate bottom curve of the glacial U trough; *C–C,* present profile.

Below. Cross profile from El Capitan to the Cathedral Rocks. Depth of glacial excavation, 900 feet. *A–A,* Preglacial profile; *B–B,* approximate bottom curve of the glacial U trough; *C–C,* present profile.

thus able to trench deeply. Bridalveil Creek, less advantageously situated, carved only a short, steeply descending gulch, which now ends abruptly at the precipice of Bridalveil Fall. That cataract, however, was not yet in existence, for the gulch led directly to the bottom of the main chasm. The present lip of the gulch at the top of the waterfall indicates roughly the level at which the Merced lay in early Quaternary time— that is, just before the first great extension of the glaciers of the Ice Age.

As it is the deepness of the "three-story" canyon—that is, the combined depths (about 3,000 feet) of the Quaternary gorge and the Pliocene and Miocene valleys above it—that gives the great trench worn by the Merced its present canyon-like character, it seems appropriate to refer to this last stage in the cutting of the Merced Canyon as the canyon stage. The reconstructed landscape of the Yosemite region in the canyon stage, as it appeared just before the advent of the glaciers of the Ice Age, is portrayed in plate 4.

There can be no doubt that the preglacial Yosemite had the proportions of a canyon rather than a valley. Its depth was 2,400 feet, measured from the brow of El Capitan, and thence decreased gradually to 2,000 feet opposite Glacier Point. However, there is to be added the height of the hills on the upland, between which the original broad valley of Miocene time lay. The depth of the canyon thus measured averaged close to 3,000 feet. As the width from rim to rim was less than the present width, the ratio of depth to width was almost the same as it is today.

The inner gorge of Yosemite, according to the testimony of the hanging valleys of the second group, was 1,500 feet deep at El Portal and 1,200 feet deep opposite Fireplace Bluff and thence extended with diminishing depth through the whole length of the chasm. Opposite Glacier Point it forked; the southern and shorter prong came abruptly to a head just above the mouth of Illilouette Valley, and the northern and longer prong extended for five miles up Tenaya Creek.

The narrowness of the preglacial canyon was accentuated by numerous craggy spurs. These were the same spurs that existed in the mountain-valley stage, but they were more rugged and more angular in outline because of the increased depth of the chasm and the development of sharp-cut ravines and gulches. The massive spur of the Cathedral Rocks now attained its greatest length—one and a half miles. It had acquired its third and lowest summit and, as its east side was gashed by deep ravines, its three summits began to stand out, severed from one another by gaps. The slender spur from which the Leaning Tower was to be carved also attained its greatest length; between it and the Cathedral Rocks, Bridalveil Creek was actively cutting its steep, V-shaped gulch all the way to the river.

The general style of modeling of the other spurs in the Yosemite Canyon may be likewise inferred, as the structure of the rock, which controlled the modeling, is indicated in the present rock forms. The front of El Capitan, from the brow down, was carved probably in short, massive buttresses; the south side of the valley immediately opposite was dissected into a number of long, sharp-crested, forking spurs. The great spur that projected from Eagle Peak was doubtless asymmetric. It fell off abruptly and irregularly toward the east and sloped smoothly and at a fairly constant angle toward the west. The spur which now ends in the sheer face of Sentinel Rock probably bore on its declining crest a series of pinnacles and crags. The spur under Glacier Point was in all probability rounded and massive, though in some places castellated like the present cliffs east of Union Point.

The long spur that projected from the base of Half Dome westward into the head of the canyon is difficult to picture, for nothing of it remains today. Yet the mere fact that the glaciers were able to destroy it throws light on the structure of the rock of which it was composed. That rock must have been thoroughly fractured, or jointed, and it may be inferred, therefore, that the spur sloped evenly, undiversified by pinnacles, knobs, or buttresses.

Half Dome itself doubtless already possessed some features that foreshadowed its present unique configuration. The back probably was already in large part smoothly rounded and bare; perhaps the crown was bare also, but the great cliff face on the northwest side was yet to be hewn out, and in its place there was a craggy, splintered slope. Half Dome then stood about 3,800 high above the point of confluence of Tenaya Creek and the Merced and already was the highest and most remarkable eminence in the immediate vicinity of the chasm.

The Little Yosemite in this stage was not much deeper than in the preceding, for the Merced had carved its inner gorge but a short distance beyond the mouth of Illilouette Valley, and from this point upstream it had accomplished little cutting because of the exceedingly resistant nature of the rock. The river at that time doubtless descended from the Little Yosemite not by successive leaps as it does today, but by a long chain of cascades. The descent amounted to 1,000 feet in a distance of about three miles.

The valley of Tenaya Creek was rapidly assuming the depth and aspect of a canyon, for though Tenaya Creek was inferior to the Merced in volume and cutting power, its cutting was greatly facilitated by a zone of closely fractured rock. Thus, even before the coming of the glaciers, Tenaya Creek approached the Yosemite through a deeper valley than that of the Merced.

Tenaya Creek, however, was the only tributary stream that was able to cut to such great depth. The other tributary streams had hanging valleys from the mouths of which they cascaded steeply into the main canyon. Even Illilouette Creek and Indian Creek, which in the mountain-valley stage had cut their valleys to the level of the master stream, now tumbled precipitously from the brink of the inner gorge. Illilouette Creek, emptying near the head of the gorge, had a cascade of only 600 feet, but Indian Creek had a chain of cascades falling 1,000 feet.

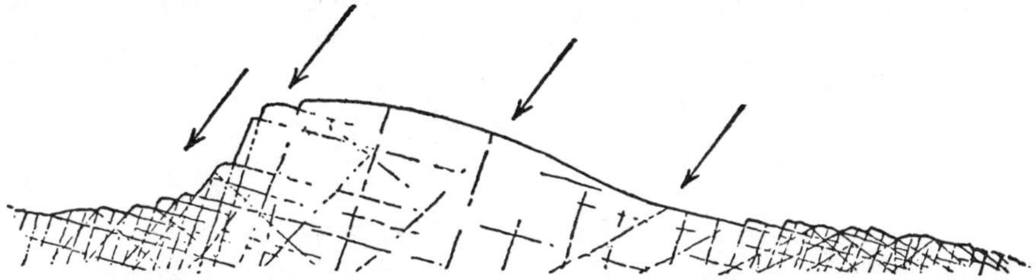

Fig. 6. Longitudinal section of a typical *roche moutonnée* fashioned by a glacier from an obdurate mass of sparsely jointed granite. The glacier moved from right to left and exerted its force in the direction indicated approximately by the arrows—that is, at a high angle against the back and crown of the hump but at a slight angle away from the downstream face. It consequently subjected the back and crown to vigorous abrasion, leaving them smoothed and gently curved, and it subjected the downstream face to quarrying mainly, leaving it hackled and abrupt. If glaciation had continued until all the jointed, quarriable rock had been removed from the downstream side, there would have resulted an asymmetric dome, smoothed on all sides but steeper on the downstream side than on the upstream side. An example of such a completely smoothed *roche moutonnée* of massive granite is the small nameless dome that stands in the Little Yosemite about half a mile northeast of Liberty Cap.

Yosemite Creek, Ribbon Creek, and the other streams of the upper set of hanging valleys had much higher cascades than in the preceding stage, owing to the added depth of the inner gorge. Some of them probably made two cascades in succession, an upper from the upland to the bottom of the old mountain valley, and a lower from the brink of the inner gorge to the river. Their measurements were as follows: Yosemite Cascade, 1,900 feet; Ribbon Cascade, 2,400 feet; Meadow Brook Cascade, 2,300 feet; Bridalveil Cascade, 1,800 feet; Sentinel Cascade, 2,400 feet.

Spectacular as these lofty cascades doubtless were, they did not add so much to the beauty of the landscape as the present leaping falls, for they descended through narrow, sharply incised gulches flanked by craggy spurs. The gulch through which Bridalveil Creek now cascades to the brink of its great fall is the only one of these preglacial gulches that remains well preserved. It is probably representative of the entire category, as it has suffered but slight change by glaciation.

About a million years ago came that epoch of wintry climate, the Great Ice Age. In the upper valleys of the Sierra Nevada, snow gathered to depths of thousands of feet and, becoming compacted to granular ice,

formed glaciers—tongue-shaped ice streams moving from a few inches
to several feet each day. The glaciers extended for scores of miles down
the main canyons, superseding the streams as valley-cutting agents.

The ancient glaciers, although they no longer exist in the Yosemite
region, can be reconstructed from the records they left in the form of
moraines (deposits of ice-borne debris), erratic boulders, and grooved
and polished rock surfaces. Not only are the position, shape, and dimensions of each ice stream definitely indicated, but also the slope and to
some extent the configuration of its surface. Hence one can form a fairly
clear conception of the character of these ice bodies and their appearance
in the landscape.

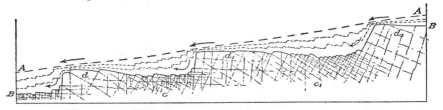

Fig. 7. Longitudinal section of a canyon illustrating the mode of development of a glacial
stairway by selective quarrying. *A–A* represents the profile of the preglacial canyon floor; *B–B*
that of the glacial stairway. Bodies of closely jointed rock, such as c and c_1, are readily quarried out by the glacier, but bodies of sparsely jointed, unquarriable rock, such as d and d_1,
being reducible only by abrasion, remain standing as obstructions with flatttened and
smoothed tops and steep, more or less hackled fronts. The broken lines indicate successive
stages in the development of the steps and treads. The arrows indicate the direction of ice
movement.

The Ice Age consisted not of one uninterrupted reign of glacial conditions but of several glacial times, each of which was hundreds of centuries
long and was separated from the others by equally long or even longer
intervals of warm climate during which the glaciers melted back part
way or all the way to their sources. The Yosemite Valley, so far as is now
known, was invaded by the ice three separate times.

Of the earliest ice advance, evidence is found in lines of large erratic
boulders scattered at levels about 200 feet above the moraines of the
second glacial stage, notably near the western base of Sentinel Dome,
700 feet above Glacier Point, and on the broad divide east of Mount
Starr King. From these boulders this glacial advance has been named
the Glacier Point stage.

Now rounded and crumbling from agelong weathering, the boulders
are the only obvious traces of what may once have been well-formed
morainal ridges. Their preservation is due to the fact that they rest on
ground which is only gently sloping, in contrast to the steep slopes below.
As the last vestiges of deposits left by Yosemite's most ancient glaciers,
marking the highest ice flood ever attained by those glaciers—which not

only engulfed the valley but overwhelmed Glacier Point and rode high on the flanks of Sentinel Dome—these boulders tell a dramatic story. So fragmentary is the record of this earliest glaciation, which ended perhaps three-quarters of a million years ago, that no pictorial restoration of the conditions then prevailing in the Yosemite region has been attempted.

The second glacial stage, though it was several hundred thousand years ago, is more fully recorded, although mainly by moraines that are now relatively obscure and partly demolished. They indicate that the Yosemite Glacier then extended to a point a short distance below El Portal, in the lower Merced Canyon. This glaciation has, accordingly, been named the El Portal stage

The evidence for the antiquity of the moraines of the second glaciation may be viewed from Glacier Point, where—on the slopes below the hotel, in the hollow to the west, and most significantly, on the wooded slopes above—glacial material is abundant. It is spread out in a sheet that scarcely suggests distinct morainal ridges, yet its glacial origin is proved by the presence of rocks foreign to the spot and known to be derived from the Little Yosemite and the High Sierra. These deposits, extending up the slopes above Glacier Point to 7,700 feet, are indubitable proof that in this glaciation the ice once rose 500 feet above the promontory.

In the lower part of Yosemite, the moraines marking the farthest limits reached by the ice are covered almost throughout with forest and brush, and in places are washed away. On the south side of the valley, the Pohono Trail crosses the highest moraine at 6,300 feet, or 2,400 feet above the valley floor. Below it are other relatively dim moraines, across which the trail zigzags to the Wawona Road. The road itself passes through glacial deposits of this age for more than a mile southwestward from Inspiration Point.

North of Yosemite Valley, moraines are preserved in a number of places. The slope between North Dome and Basket Dome is veneered with old glacial debris up to 7,600 feet; and the trail from North Dome to Indian Creek crosses several extensive moraine-covered areas.

An excellent locality in which to search out ancient moraines is the slope on the north side of the Little Yosemite, which is traversed by the trails to Half Dome and Clouds Rest, at altitudes of about 7,250 to over 8,000 feet. In the deeper trail cuts and in holes left by uprooted trees, boulders and cobbles of typical glacial forms protrude from the superficial blanket of sand and soil. As the traveler proceeds up the slope, he realizes that it is veneered for the most part with old glacial materials. He perceives also that in many places these form indistinct swells a foot or two high that extend across the slope. These are indeed old, dim moraines that have long since lost their crests and been reduced by slow disintegration to a mere fraction of their original height. The boulders which composed them are rust-stained and weathered to a depth of an eighth of an inch to a half inch. Many are so decayed that they fall apart at a moderate blow, or are readily cut with pick or shovel.

On the south side of the Little Yosemite similar vestiges of old moraines occur at corresponding levels. They may be readily traced south

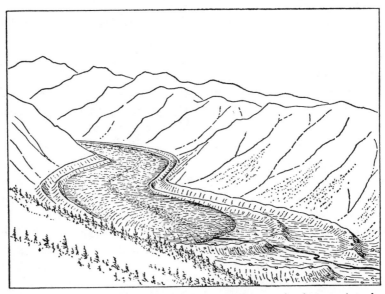

Fig. 8. Idealized sketch of glacier leaving successive moraine loops as it melts back. In the Sierra Nevada, where the glaciers carried relatively little rock debris, many of the moraines are of the sharp-crested, clean-cut type portrayed here.

of Helen Lake and in the vicinity of Starr King Meadows, where they describe great arcs. It is on this upland, perhaps, that the student may best learn to recognize the older moraines by their constituent materials as well as their indistinct forms. Having become sensitive to these characters, he may then be able to discern dim vestiges of old morainal deposits in many parts of the Yosemite region.[1]

Rock surfaces which must have been overridden by ice of the El Portal stage impress the observer by their manifold signs of age and prolonged exposure to the weather. They have lost their polish and even the smooth-flowing contours imparted by the glaciers. So roughened are they by the irregular disintegration of the rock and the eroding action of rain

---

[1] In this chapter the reader is directed to only a few of the best and most accessible localities in which he may observe the records of the various glacial stages. Plate 29, Map of Glacial and Postglacial Deposits in Yosemite Valley, accompanying Professional Paper 160, shows the exact distribution of the moraines and other glacial features.

water that one would not suspect that they had been glacially planed and polished if it were not that they are surrounded by ancient moraines.

No evidence testifies more eloquently to the antiquity of this glaciation than the glacial boulders now perched on rock pedestals several feet high. The pedestals are composed of the local rock, attached to the body of the mountain, and owe their preservation to the protection of the boulders. Since the ice deposited the boulders in their present situations, the pedestals have gradually developed, whereas the surrounding unprotected rock has disintegrated and been stripped away. Pedestals of different height were formed. Of two boulders on Moraine Dome,

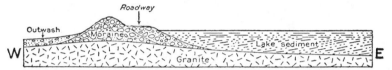

Fig. 9. Section across moraine dam at El Capitan Bridge, showing the depth to which it is believed to be buried under lake sediment on the upstream side and under outwash material on the downstream side.

one has a one-foot pedestal, the other a three-foot pedestal. On the mountain west of Upper Yosemite Fall is a boulder standing on a five-foot pedestal, the highest in the region.

The pedestals do not afford accurate measures of the total depth of stripping effected since glaciation, but on the very summit of Moraine Dome is a remarkable feature which gives more dependable information. Here (incidentally, near one perched boulder and another that has been dethroned from its pedestal) is a dike of aplite—that is, a sheet of fine-grained rock that invaded a vertical fissure in the granite. The dike now stands prominently in relief, seven feet high at the highest point, like a stone wall partly fallen in ruins. (See fig. 11.) It owes its prominence to the fact that aplite, which is exceedingly resistant to weathering, has remained while the surrounding rock has disintegrated and been stripped away.

Now it is not conceivable that the aplite wall was in existence at the time of the earlier glaciation, for the ice then passed over Moraine Dome with a thickness of 500 feet and with sufficient power to raze all such frail projections. Indeed, when the ice withdrew, the aplite dike was doubtless planed off even with the surrounding granite. There can be no doubt, then, that the aplite wall has been etched out since the time of the glaciation, and its height, seven feet, is a conservative measure of the reduction in height which bare eminences such as Moraine Dome have suffered since the climax of the ice flood. On the sloping south side of the crown of Moraine Dome are two other wall-like features, both consisting of masses of granite preserved under steeply inclined dikes of aplite. These stand in relief eight and twelve feet respectively. The stripping which etched them out was evidently more rapid because of the slope.

From the evidence of its moraines, the Yosemite Glacier of the El Portal stage can be reliably reconstructed. The Yosemite region as it then appeared is shown in plate 5. From its sources in the High Sierra, the great Yosemite Glacier extended westward a distance of thirty-seven miles and filled Yosemite Valley to the brim, winding its way through it like a broad, majestic river. In the valley it had an average width of two miles, but in its lower course it expanded to almost double that breadth. Its greatest thickness was opposite Glacier Point, more than 3,000 feet, and over Bridalveil Meadow, 2,500 feet. Its terminus, below El Portal, lay at an altitude of 2,000 feet.

By this ice flood Half Dome was deeply immersed, but its crown rose 700 feet above the ice and was never overwhelmed. So great was the congestion of ice caused by the bottleneck between North Dome and Glacier Point that the abrupt increase in depth at the head of Yosemite Valley made no significant break in the surface of the ice. Glacier Point was covered by the ice, but Sentinel Dome, a mile back, was not overridden. From Glacier Point westward the surface of the Yosemite Glacier probably declined evenly. Along this stretch the ice nowhere spilled over the upland on the south side of the valley, even during the culminating phases of glaciation, but it did not fall far short of reaching the brink, for it passed completely over the Cathedral Rocks. It filled the lower gulch of Bridalveil Creek, where it was joined by a small tributary glacier from the south, and it passed westward over the summit of the Leaning Tower. This entire group of features, now so conspicuous, was submerged by the sea of ice. Along the north margin of the glacier, Eagle Peak was the first sharp *nunatak,* or "island" of rock, to split the ice sea, but a short distance farther west rose the bare, rounded crowns of El Capitan and Boundary Ridge.

Vast as the Yosemite Glacier was at this time, it was but a moderately large ice stream for the Sierra Nevada. Its neighbors to the north and the south, the Tuolumne Glacier and the San Joaquin Glacier, each attained a length of about sixty miles.

The third and most recent stage of the Ice Age, termed the Wisconsin (after the midwestern state which at this time became mantled with glacial deposits left by the continental ice sheet), is well documented by many well-preserved, sharp-crested moraines containing a large proportion of unweathered granite boulders, as well as by the polished and grooved rock surfaces which are conspicuous in parts of the Yosemite region, especially in the High Sierra.

In the lower Yosemite, six frontal moraines occur within the distance of a mile. The lowermost is immediately above Bridalveil Meadow. Being widely breached by the Merced River, it consists of two short segments, one on the south side of the valley, the other on the north side. The southern segment is readily identified as a massive wooded ridge about 40 feet high that extends northwestward and breaks off abruptly at the bank of the river. The northern segment consists of a narrower and sharper-crested ridge that extends southwestward to the edge of the northern motor road, where it also breaks off abruptly.

The materials of this moraine may be readily inspected in the road cuts. Most conspicuous are the large, smoothly rounded boulders, but mixed with these are angular rock fragments of different sizes, and an abundance of sand and mud. Many of the boulders and cobbles, when washed and held in the sunlight, appear highly polished and in places scratched or scored like the glaciated canyon floors of the High Sierra. This is proof that they have been brought down by a glacier, that they are glacier-worn as well as stream-worn, for, though their roundness is due largely to stream wear, their polish could have been imparted only by long-continued glacial abrasion. To the trained eye of the geologist, moreover, it is readily apparent that the deposit contains some types of rock that are foreign to the Yosemite region but are prevalent in the High Sierra. These characteristics, together with the forms and position of the ridges, bespeak the glacial origin of the deposits.

The second and third moraines are even more widely breached than the first; indeed, they are largely demolished. Of the fourth moraine, by contrast, the principal remnant projects boldly from the northwestern base of the Cathedral Rocks in the form of a stony, scantily timbered ridge about 30 feet high.

Of greatest interest are the fifth and sixth moraines, which together form a nearly straight dam across the valley just below El Capitan Meadow. Only a small gap interrupts the continuity of this dam—the gap cut by the river and now spanned by El Capitan Bridge. North of the bridge the road is laid upon the sixth moraine, as upon a causeway raised a few feet above the level of the meadow.

Above El Capitan Bridge, no further moraines are to be found for about five miles—that is, to a point near the head wall of the valley. There, however, is the largest and most conspicuous moraine of all—a hummocky ridge 50 to 60 feet high and half a mile long that extends from the head wall directly down the middle of the valley and declines gradually to the level of the valley floor at Clark Bridge. The road that leads from the Happy Isles to Mirror Lake passes through a saddle in this ridge. From the cut have been taken many rounded and polished boulders of various rock types from the High Sierra. The faint curvature of the ridge, concave toward the north, suggests that it is the remnant of a moraine loop left by the Tenaya Glacier.

In Tenaya Canyon itself moraines are virtually lacking, owing primarily to the excessive steepness and smoothness of its walls. But in the Little Yosemite Valley moraines are plentiful, and form an orderly system, rich in lateral and frontal moraines and including several almost complete loops. The regular spacing of some of these moraines, very evident when their distribution is indicated on a map, is remarkable, and justifies the inference that the recurring fluctuations of the declining Merced Glacier were essentially periodic.

On the north side of the Little Yosemite Valley the Sunrise Trail zigzags across the entire series of lateral moraines. Impressive even to the casual observer is the prevalence of large blocks in these moraines. Most blocks are imperfectly rounded, their edges and corners having been blunted and worn smooth in the course of their long journey on and in the ice; but there are some sharply angular, clean-cut blocks that appear to have suffered almost no wear since the day when they were torn from the cliffs. The traveler is impressed by the great abundance of fresh-looking, essentially unweathered blocks, which ring when struck with a hammer and give every proof of being composed of sound, hard granite—this despite the fact that they have lain exposed to the weather for certainly not less than 10,000 years, those in the highest moraines of the series probably several times this period.

Moraines of this stage also cling to the north and south flanks of Moraine Dome. North of the Dome a succession of moraines is crossed by the Soda Springs Trail. On the south side of the Dome the topmost and largest moraine, which spirals around the mountain, is conspicuous in the landscape because of the strip of forest that sets it off from the barren rock slopes above and below. It is, indeed, for this remarkable embankment that the dome is named.

Traced several miles to the northeast, these moraines form another great series of parallel crests and terraces at the south end of Sunrise Mountain. Here they attain great volume and superb development, many of them resembling artificial embankments, evenly graded and laid out in smooth curves. The topmost moraine is the largest and most impressive. It bears on its crest a row of granite blocks which, shimmering white through the dark foliage of the trees, produces the effect in a distant view of a chalk line drawn across the mountainside to mark the highest level reached by the ice.[2]

---

[2] The two sets of moraines on either side of the Little Yosemite Valley must have been deposited by two ice floods, separated by an interval during which the glacier melted down

Such, then, are the evidences of the third glaciation. The ice bodies which the moraines so clearly outline may now be reconstructed. (See pl. 6.) Yosemite Valley was occupied by an ice stream of moderate dimensions, which filled the valley to only one-third of its depth and, as is attested by its moraines, reached a little below El Capitan and Bridalveil Fall. It was formed wholly by the confluence of the two great ice streams that issued from Tenaya Canyon and the Little Yosemite Valley.

The Tenaya Glacier sloped evenly to join the trunk glacier in Yosemite Valley without a break. In contrast, the Merced Glacier tumbled from the mouth of the Little Yosemite in magnificent chaos, down the giant stairway whose great steps are now marked by Nevada Fall and Vernal Fall, and plunged over the sheer front of Mount Broderick and through the gaps on either side. Broken into fantastic blades and pinnacles (*séracs*), the cascading portion of the glacier must have presented the appearance of a tumultuous cataract frozen into immobility. The even, compact ice mass that lay below in Yosemite Valley must have resembled a deep, tranquil pool.

Where the two ice streams joined, at the head of the valley, the Yosemite Glacier was about 1,500 feet thick, but down the valley it diminished so that in the portal opposite the Cathedral Rocks it was only 400 to 500 feet thick. Throughout the greater part of its course the surface of the glacier sloped gently and evenly, but at the upper end as well as at the terminus it sloped more steeply.

The ice surface reached almost to the shoulder above the Royal Arches; it was about level with the rock platform above Lower Yosemite Fall and lay just below Columbia Rock. On the south side of the valley Glacier Point towered fully 2,000 feet above the glacier; Union Point rose about 1,000 feet above it, and even the Cathedral Spires stood entirely clear, the ice reaching barely to the base of the lower spire. Bridalveil Fall, then as now, leaped from its 600-foot precipice, but its lower portion probably disappeared in an abyss which the waters had melted in the side of the glacier.

The Yosemite Glacier must have presented the appearance of a fairly clean ice stream—much cleaner than most of its contemporaries in the Cascade Range or the Rocky Mountains, for the granitic rocks of the Yosemite region and the adjoining High Sierra, being not only hard but tough and prevailingly massive, yielded much less debris to the pass-

---

to a relatively low level or withdrew from the valley altogether. The third, or Wisconsin, glacial stage was evidently characterized by two glacial maxima, or substages. The interval between them was not long, however, for the deposits of the first ice flood look but little older than those produced by the second. There is an abundance of confirmatory evidence in the moraine series in other valleys of the Sierra Nevada.

ing ice streams than did the well-jointed and less coherent rocks in other regions. Nevertheless, the Yosemite Glacier was not a dazzling white *mer de glace* throughout. Its margins were littered with large blocks and smaller fragments of granite, and along its middle extended a medial moraine which resulted from the junction of the Merced and the Tenaya glaciers.

Doubtless this medial moraine was one of the glacier's striking features. Beginning at the head of the valley as a narrow dirt band, it broadened gradually, assuming the form of a low, hummocky ridge on the back of the glacier. The clean lanes on either side of the medial moraine became narrower toward the glacier's terminus and eventually vanished, as the entire surface became mantled with debris.

The ice front itself varied in character as it oscillated. During periods of advance it was abrupt and wall-like; in periods of recession it sloped at a moderate angle; and when stationary for any length of time it probably was not clearly distinguishable from the moraine. As the glacier finally melted back toward the head of the valley, meltwater was ponded in the basin it had formed, so that a lake came into existence. The front of the glacier, being immersed in the lake, was kept sheer by the breaking off of ice masses that floated about as small icebergs.

The two earlier ice invasions, being the more extensive, were also the more effective in remodeling the landscape. The latest ice invasion accomplished relatively little excavation, but it did accentuate the glaciated character of the upper part of the valley. Each glacial stage superimposed its changes on those wrought at earlier stages, so that differentiation is difficult or impossible. It is the cumulative changes of the Ice Age which concern us.

When the reign of ice at length came to an end, Yosemite Valley no longer presented the appearance of a narrow "three-story" canyon. Both downward and sideward the glaciers had quarried, trimming projecting spurs, cutting back the craggy slopes of the preglacial river canyon to sheer, smooth cliffs, and transforming the cascades descending from the hanging side valleys into the present leaping falls of astounding height. (See chap. 8.) The reconstructed landscape of the Yosemite region, as it appeared just after the Ice Age, is depicted in plate 7.

Throughout the length of the valley the inner gorge of the Merced was wiped out, and in its stead was produced a broadly concave, basin-shaped rock floor. Even the features of the mountain-valley stage were largely destroyed, and thus from a tortuous V canyon the Yosemite was enlarged to a spacious, moderately sinuous U trough with parallel, spurless sides and with a basin scooped out in the rock floor of the valley, in which was formed a lake—the now extinct Lake Yosemite.

Only between El Capitan and the Cathedral Rocks, where there were massive rocks which the glacier could not quarry away, did it leave a marked constriction. In the areas of sparsely jointed granite immediately above and below Yosemite Valley the ice was able to effect only moderate changes in the form of the canyon. There, in consequence, the inner gorge of the Merced preserves the characteristics of a trench worn by the river in the bottom of an old mountain valley.

In Yosemite Valley the depth of glacial excavation decreases from a maximum of about 1,500 feet at the head to a minimum of about 500 feet at the lower end. This decrease in glacial deepening down the valley is due to the fact that throughout all phases of glaciation the ice was thicker and therefore had greater excavating power at the head of the valley than at the lower end, and during the maximum phases it plunged into the head of the valley in the form of a mighty ice cataract.

At the mouth of the Little Yosemite, the glacier sculptured the steps of the giant stairway from local bodies of extremely massive rock. Quarrying headward directly up to the vertical master joints delimiting those bodies and grinding them down from above, the glacier gave them their marvelously clean-cut, steplike forms. Through the hewing of this stairway, two new falls came into existence as the Merced descended the steps in two successive leaps—Nevada Fall and Vernal Fall. (A third new fall was created in Yosemite Valley itself, for in deepening the chasm the glaciers had left the gulch of Bridalveil Creek hanging.)

In the lower half of the Little Yosemite, lateral quarrying was favored, but downward quarrying was impeded by the structure of the rocks; that part of the valley was thus given great breadth but relatively little depth. The Little Yosemite, the path of the master stream, now lies anomalously 2,000 feet higher than Tenaya Canyon, which is the path of a feeble tributary. Liberty Cap and Mount Broderick, being composed almost wholly of massive rock which could not be quarried, were left standing at its mouth as two gigantic *roches moutonnées* ("sheep backs"). The upper half of the Little Yosemite was, like the head of the main Yosemite, the site of a powerful ice cataract, and to that circumstance owes its great depth and peculiar configuration. In the Little Yosemite, as in the main Yosemite, the depth of glacial excavation decreases steadily down the valley, and for the same reasons.

In Tenaya Canyon, downward quarrying was favored by the presence of a longitudinal belt of fractures, but lateral quarrying was restricted by flanking masses of undivided rock. As a consequence, that canyon was cut down almost to the level of the Yosemite and was given even greater depth than Yosemite Valley, but it was comparatively narrow and in part shaped like a sharp-keeled boat rather than a U trough. Only an imperfect stairway was developed in its floor, but at its head a gigantic step was fashioned from a body of massive granite under the cascading action of the glacier.

Lake basins like that of Lake Yosemite, but smaller and shallower, were scooped out in both the Little Yosemite and Tenaya Canyon.

The Yosemite, the Little Yosemite, and Tenaya Canyon, then, owe their present configuration largely to glacial action. All three had been cut in preglacial time to considerable depth by the streams flowing through them and had acquired the aspect of rugged V canyons, but so thoroughgoing was the remodeling action of the glaciers that only a few vestiges of their preglacial forms remain. Each chasm had a glacial cataract at its head, yet the three chasms differ in shape and proportions because of their differing rock structure.

The great cliffs and domes of Yosemite are made of massive granite. El Capitan and the Cathedral Rocks project from the walls of the valley because they consist of enormous monoliths that yielded but little to the onslaughts of the ice. Half Dome and the other domes rise high in the landscape because their unfractured masses have survived the destruction wrought by ice and weather in the surrounding fractured rock. They owe their smoothly rounded forms not to the grinding of overriding glaciers—some have never been overridden—but to the curious bursting of concentric layers, or "shells," from their surfaces.

Since the Ice Age ended, there have been only a few noteworthy changes in the aspect of the Yosemite region. The shallow lake basins in the Little Yosemite and Tenaya canyons were gradually filled by the forward-growing deltas which the streams built with their loads of sand and gravel. Merced River and Tenaya Creek filled the larger and deeper basin of Lake Yosemite, and the level, parklike valley floor was created. The cliffs have suffered from the destructive action of the elements, which has piled up at their feet great masses of rock waste. Huge rock avalanches, some thrown down probably by earthquakes, have dammed Tenaya Canyon at its mouth, impounding Mirror Lake. Other great rock slides in the lower half of the valley formed long slopes that have permitted man to build roads to the uplands.

At present the Merced is further deepening its canyon, the cliffs are being sculptured by frost and heat and rain, and almost imperceptible changes are taking place even on the face of El Capitan, which seemingly stands as eternal as the "Rock of Ages."

5

The sculpturing of the walls

The Yosemite owes its distinctive cliff sculpture to the unusual and varied rock structure. The sparsely jointed granites have given rise to high, smooth cliffs; and the more closely jointed rocks have been sculptured into angular, faceted forms, in which the controlling influence of master joints trending in different directions is evident.[1] Narrow zones of intensely shattered rock, particularly vulnerable to the weathering processes, have been etched out here and there, giving rise to variously shaped recesses, clefts, and gulches. Rock remnants of sufficient structural strength survive as pinnacles and larger monuments. And the larger bodies of undivided, massive granite, by the progressive casting off of concentric shells from their surfaces, have become smoothly rounded domes.

Joints, then, are of supreme importance in understanding the sculpturing of Yosemite's walls. Not only does the arrangement of joints differ

[1] The formation of joints is considered in chapter 1, pages 54–55.

from place to place, but the spacing varies widely. In certain zones the joints are only a few inches apart, and the rock is shattered into small slabs or mere slivers. Elsewhere and more commonly the intervals between joints range from a foot to a score of feet, so that the rock is divided into great angular blocks or thick sheets. In other places there are no joints for hundreds and even thousands of feet, and the rock is wholly undivided. These variations are in places remarkably abrupt, so that structural extremes are brought into immediate juxtaposition. In few other regions where granitic rocks occur are there so great structural diversities or so many sharp contrasts as in the Yosemite region. And to these factors, in large measure, may be attributed the seemingly unlimited variety of patterns into which the natural agencies have sculptured Yosemite's walls.

These facts became evident to the author in 1905, while he was engaged in the topographic surveys for the map of Yosemite Valley. The very task of delineating the cliffs in detail drew his attention to the relationship between their sculpture and their inner structure.

But why such variety and such wide extremes within a relatively small area? The answer to the question was not wholly clear until a colleague, Frank C. Calkins, in 1913 showed that the chasm is situated in an exceptional locality where many small bodies of igneous rock (the relatively basic ones, granodiorite, diorite, and gabbro) have been intruded into the otherwise vast, unbroken bodies of siliceous granite and monzonite that make up the central parts of the great granitic area (batholith) of the Sierra Nevada; and that these basic rocks are more closely jointed than the siliceous rocks.

A detailed account of the rocks of Yosemite is beyond the scope of this book, but the following quotation from Calkins[2] will give a general picture:

At first glance the walls and domes of the Yosemite region appear to be formed of one and the same kind of rock, for they present no striking variations in color suggestive of different rock types. Gray tints prevail throughout, and it is difficult even for a discerning observer to tell at a distance in what measure the differences in shade are expressive of differences in rock composition and in what measure they are due merely to the varied distribution of the lichens that grow on the surface of the rocks. In reality, however, there are present in the Yosemite region about a dozen distinct types of rock, all granitic and ranging in color from nearly white through gray to nearly black; but so universal is the mottled effect produced by the lichens that the contrasts

[2] The rocks of the Yosemite region are fully described in the Appendix which Calkins contributed to *Geologic History of the Yosemite Valley*, Professional Paper 160, U. S. Geological Survey (Washington, D.C., 1930). The geologic map which accompanies the Appendix (pl. 51) shows the distribution of the rocks. The quotation is from Calkin's Appendix.

in rock color are greatly subdued, or even completely obscured, especially on the little-sunned northward-facing cliffs, on which the lichens form an almost continuous veneer. . . . Nevertheless, the walls of the Yosemite Valley afford an exceptionally instructive field for the student of igneous intrusion: In few places elsewhere can he behold in cross section a more remarkable complex of intrusive bodies.

Of course it is not possible to determine exactly the original extent within the valley area of each of the masses of well-jointed basic rocks, as most of them have been removed by erosion, and the rock floor of the valley is hidden from view by a thick deposit of sand and gravel. However, numerous remnants of the basic rocks are visible in the walls and on the adjoining uplands. From a detailed survey of these remnants it is possible to estimate the original extent of the intrusive bodies and to appraise the effect they must have had on the quarrying action of the glaciers. Indeed, enough is known to account satisfactorily for the development of all the major features of the Yosemite region: for the division of Yosemite Valley into two broad chambers; for its peculiar spoon-shaped lower end and its equally peculiar square upper end; for the stepwise ascent of the giant stairway; for the breadth of the Little Yosemite and the depth of Tenaya Canyon—and to provide a sound basis for interpreting the features graven in Yosemite's walls.

By no means all the detail is of postglacial origin. Much of it was produced during the latest stage of glaciation, when the valley was filled with ice to only one-third of its depth and when its cliffs were exposed to intense frost action and frequent wear by snow avalanches. Much of the sculpturing dates also from the relatively long interglacial stage that preceded; the deeper recesses doubtless were initiated long before the Ice Age, while the Yosemite was passing through the mountain-valley and canyon stages of its earlier development. Nevertheless, all its sculptured features may appropriately be treated together here, the purpose being to explain how they were formed rather than to trace their origins.

Sentinel Rock is an outstanding example of the relationship of form to structure. Its sheer, smooth cliff is determined largely by a single nearly vertical joint plane. The granodiorite of which it is formed has a sheeted structure; the nearly vertical joints, which have a northeastward trend, are developed to the exclusion of almost all the joints in other directions. The influence of the northeasterly joints is evident also in the splintered crest of the spur of which Sentinel Rock forms part, in the sculpture of the rock mass at its base, in the steps over which Sentinel Creek cascades, and in the truncated spurs for some distance along the south side of the valley.

In the neighborhood of Taft Point, oblique joints dipping 40°–50°

W. begin to influence the cliff sculpture, so that the spurs are conspicuously asymmetric. The sloping west side of each spur coincides with one or more oblique joint planes; the precipitous east side is defined by a northwest-trending vertical master joint; and the point is truncated by a sheer facet of the northeasterly joint system. All the minor sculptural features that diversify the spurs are similarly bounded by fractures of the three sets mentioned and are of asymmetric, rhombic pattern. Even stream erosion is here guided by structural planes. The streamlet that descends the asymmetric gorge east of Profile Cliff cuts not vertically but obliquely, sliding sidewise, so to speak, along the plane of an inclined master joint. The overhang of Profile Cliff and of the entire west wall of the gorge is due to the undercutting action of the streamlet.

The astounding fissures that gash the overhanging wall and edge of the gorge near Profile Cliff have developed along vertical joints of the northeasterly system. Probably the rock immediately adjacent to these partings was peculiarly susceptible to weathering, having been minutely sheared and slivered by faulting movements that took place under great pressure soon after the granite had solidified. The joints, which were at first mere cracks too narrow for a knife blade to enter, have become enlarged to gaping abysses too wide for a man to stride across. Their enlargement is the more surprising in view of the fact that no streams have ever made their way through them, since the surface of the upland here slopes to the west, away from the edge of the gorge.

Oblique master joints, dipping to the west, account also for the asymmetric forms of the Cathedral Rocks. Eastward-dipping joints determine the angle of the rock slope on the west side of Bridalveil Creek. The V-shaped gulch of that stream owes its wonderful symmetry to the fact that the oblique joints controlling the inclination of each of its two sides dip toward one another at approximately the same angle. The finest example of asymmetric sculpture called forth by oblique master joints is presented by the massif of the Three Brothers. Its three successive roofs slant with architectural regularity at a uniform angle, because they are determined by joint planes having the same westerly dip. The gables, however, are carved along vertical joint planes trending northeastward.

In the embayment east of the Cathedral Rocks, where diorite and gabbro are the prevailing rocks, the jointing is intricate and irregular. The wall of the valley here is so thoroughly dissected by deep, ramifying gulches that it is reduced to a bewildering mass of craggy, slivered spurs. Some of the outstanding pinnacles consist of granite, sheets of which cut through the other rocks. Of this resistant and relatively massive granite are made also the twin shafts of the Cathedral Spires, which alone have survived the dismantling that has taken place about them.

In the lower Yosemite chamber, vertical joints predominate. Exclusive control by eastward- and northward-trending vertical joints is seen in the sheer square-cut cliffs that frame the recess of Ribbon Fall. Easterly and northerly joints, combined with northeasterly and northwesterly joints, have influenced the shaping of the cliffs on the south side. So strong has been their directive control that in several places, notably below Crocker Point, the cliffs have been quarried back by the glaciers and have since been chiseled in detail irrespective of the positions of the drainage lines on the slopes above. In the Merced Gorge, northwest- and northeast-trending joints of approximately equal strength have given rise to the clean-cut prismatic forms along the edge of Turtleback Dome.

In the upper Yosemite chamber the most impressive example of a rock face determined by a single master joint is found in the great cliff at Glacier Point. Though not without minor irregularities, it coincides throughout most of its height and length with one vertical joint plane trending almost due east. The projecting slabs at its top are explained by the local development of horizontal fractures that interfere with the continuity of the vertical master joint. They were left overhanging when the last vertical rock sheet fell from the cliff face.

Below the main cliff at Glacier Point is a second even higher cliff (about 1,200 feet), also defined by an eastward-trending master joint; a short distance to the west is the singularly straight, narrow cleft through which the Ledge Trail leads steeply to Glacier Point—a cleft caused by weathering and erosion along a nearly vertical master fracture, probably a fault, that traverses the rock in a southeasterly direction.

In striking contrast to these colossal rock forms are the finely chiseled, castellated, and columnar features, near Moran Point and Union Point, which have been called forth by numerous intersecting joints, vertical, oblique, and horizontal. The best-known representative of this type of sculpture is the Agassiz Column, which stands, precariously balanced on a crumbling base, near the Glacier Point Short Trail, just below and east of Union Point. Every facet of this rock is determined by a joint plane.

Very clear are the relations between sculpture and structure in the cliffs about the Yosemite Falls (see pp. 146, 147). The two bush-covered terraces to the right and the left of Lower Yosemite Fall are defined by horizontal master joints, whereas the incline west of Upper Yosemite Fall coincides with a zone of oblique master joints. These features are of peculiar human interest because, were it not for them, the building of a trail to the top of the Yosemite Falls would have been extremely difficult. As it is, the trail builder took advantage of the upper rock terrace to carry the trail from Columbia Rock to the embayment of the Upper

Fall, and constructed the upper flight of zigzags on the incline produced by the oblique joints.

The 1,500-foot precipice over which Upper Yosemite Fall leaps is determined, like the cliff at Glacier Point, by an eastward-trending master joint, which is inclined at an angle of about 80°. Only the west half, which is composed of granodiorite, approximates a plane, smooth wall; the east half, which is composed of granite, is diversified by overlapping rock sheets. A narrow ledge defined by a horizontal master joint—Muir's famous Fern Ledge—extends westward across the face to and slightly beyond the path of the fall, about 450 feet above the base. This ledge is the most advanced part of the cliff, yet it is cleared by the main body of the fall, owing to the parabolic descent of the water. Below the ledge the cliff overhangs at angles ranging from 10° to 30°, and at its base is a deep cavern developed along another horizontal master joint.

Upper Yosemite Fall has failed to carve a recess because the cliff as a whole has receded by the scaling off of immense rock sheets. The stubs of a number of these are to be seen in the projecting buttress under Yosemite Point. The most remarkable remnant of such a sheet is the gigantic tapering rock monument known as the Lost Arrow, which clings to the cliff east of the fall. It has a total height of about 1,500 feet, and its upper third stands detached, like a pinnacle, the parting behind it having been enlarged to an open cleft, doubtless as a result of the destructive action of the spray from the fall which freezes in it in winter.

All the major waterfalls of the leaping type in the Yosemite region are, like Upper Yosemite Fall, associated with a cliff determined by a vertical or nearly vertical master joint. Lower Yosemite Fall leaps over a northwest-trending cliff; Bridalveil Fall and Illilouette Fall, each over a northeast-trending cliff; Vernal Fall over a northwest-trending cliff. The precipice over which Nevada Fall descends is less clearly determined by a master joint than the others, but its straight front and northeastward trend betray the influence of a northeasterly joint plane. Being controlled by joints of different sets, the cliffs of Vernal Fall and Nevada Fall are at right angles to each other, as strikingly shows in plate 14 and on the topographic map of the valley. At nearly every fall the cliff cuts diagonally across the path of the stream and without reference to the direction in which the ancient glaciers moved: the directive control exercised by the rock structure is supreme, and its effect is unobscured by either stream or glacial erosion. The Cascades, the only major falls that are not of the leaping type, descend, however, over irregularly fractured rock that does not stand in a smooth, clean-cut wall.

Among the most puzzling features of the walls of the Yosemite are the deeply cut recesses and gulches that occur where no streams or only insignificant streamlets come down from the upland. A striking example is the capacious recess west of El Capitan, the dimensions of which are out of all proportion to the little upland vale that drains into it. Not only is it many times as large as the recess cut by Ribbon Fall, but it is larger than the embayment at Upper Yosemite Fall. Nor can it be attributed to the eroding action of a powerful torrent that came from a melting glacier on the upland during the Ice Age, for the crown of El Capitan and the hills to the north and northwest of it have never borne any ice.

Examination of the recess leaves no doubt that it has been developed in a zone of intensely fractured rock by the destructive action of ground water, frosts, torrential rains, and snowslides. Several master joints converge toward the head of the recess, which is carved in granite of the same kind as that of which the towering mass of El Capitan is composed. Between the master joints the rock is cut by a multitude of cross joints, so that even its more resistant portions stand up only in the form of a slivered, comblike crest. Rock so thoroughly broken yields more readily to the dismantling agents than the durable masses of undivided rock near by. The contrast in sculpture is accounted for by the difference in structure.

Other sharply incised recesses that are similarly etched out along narrow zones of intense fracturing separate the three summits of the Cathedral Rocks. The largest and deepest recess of this type, however, is the gulch of Eagle Creek, west of the Three Brothers. It is larger than Indian Canyon, yet, unlike that canyon, it receives no drainage from an upland valley. Like the recess west of El Capitan, it has been developed along a zone of shattering, in which the sculpturing agents—storm waters and snowslides, which converge in its funnel-like form—have worked with especial ease.

To this class of recesses belong also the mysterious notches, gulches, and alcoves cut in the lips of the hanging valleys near to but not at the waterfalls. Such are the broadly open notch west of Upper Yosemite Fall, the alcove with overhanging roof at the head of the recess into which Lower Yosemite Fall plunges, and the alcove at the head of Illilouette Gorge, which is carved in the mountainside irrespective of the position of Illilouette Fall. A similar feature occurs on the steps of the giant stairway over which the Merced River descends.

Just north of Nevada Fall is a gorge through which the tourist trail to the Little Yosemite is laid. It was cut, in all probability, by a torrent that flowed along the northern margin of the Merced Glacier at a time when that glacier still occupied the Little Yosemite but had already melted back from the lower steps of the giant stairway. However, the fact must not be disregarded that the gorge coincides with a zone of fracturing—the only zone of that kind which traverses the otherwise massive granite at the mouth of the Little Yosemite. Were it not for the presence of this favoring structure, the glacial torrent in the short period of its existence probably could not have become so deeply entrenched. No corresponding gorge exists on the south side of Nevada Fall, though doubtless there was a glacial torrent also along the southern margin of the Merced Glacier. But the granite on the south side of the valley is extremely massive, and this fact suffices to explain the absence of a gorge.

The zone of fracturing north of Nevada Fall must have facilitated glacial erosion as well as stream erosion. The selective manner in which glaciers excavate in rocks of variable structure has been explained (pp. 107–108). The most impressive product of selective action by a glacier is the deep gorge between Liberty Cap and Mount Broderick, which was excavated along a northeast-trending zone of vertical fractures. It is probable, therefore, that the gorge north of Nevada Fall was excavated in large part by the Merced Glacier and then was further deepened by the temporary glacial torrent.

6 The domes

Of all the colossal rock monuments that line Yosemite Valley, those which seem most strangely modeled are the huge, bald, helmet-shaped domes. The visitor may marvel at the height of the chasm's towering walls and spires, yet he is not altogether surprised, for angularity and cragginess seem natural in mountain sculpture. But domes, round and smooth, as if fashioned by the hand of man, he is scarcely prepared to see. Domes exist in few places on this earth and are seldom the theme of the artist's brush or pen. And so the domes have been the most baffling features of the Yosemite's extraordinary landscape.

These domes are now known to be the outstanding representatives of a whole class of forms, all distinguished by their smoothly rounded shapes and their development in unjointed, massive rocks. This class is in striking contrast to the angular, faceted types of sculpture developed in jointed rocks. In the same category as the domes, and closely allied to them, are the whaleback spurs, cylindrical ridges, conoidal buttresses, and arches. Indeed, the Yosemite region contains a greater and more varied assemblage of such distinctive forms than any other area of similar extent in the Sierra Nevada or, perhaps, on the earth.

A long-prevalent misconception, even among scientists, was that the domes are essentially gigantic *roches moutonnées,* worn round by mighty overriding glaciers. As one student expressed it, "The whole surface of the region with its greater and smaller domes had been molded beneath a universal ice sheet or confluent glacier which moved onward with a steady current careless of domes."

When this statement was made, there was no means of testing the soundness of the theory, but there is now abundant proof that the Sierra Nevada was never overwhelmed by a "universal ice sheet" but bore only glaciers of local origin. The depth to which these glaciers covered the Yosemite region is known, within a narrow margin of error, from the survey of the moraines. Several of the domes, it can be stated positively, were never overtopped by the ice of the glacial epoch: Sentinel Dome stood wholly above the highest level of glaciation; all the bare, dome-like part of Mount Starr King has remained untouched by the ice; and the crown of Half Dome rose like a rocky isle fully 500 feet above the surface of the Merced and the Tenaya glaciers, which coalesced about it. Yet these domes are among the most conspicuous and most typical domes of the Yosemite region.

That glacial abrasion is not a necessary factor in the development of domes is demonstrated, further, by the fact that the celebrated Stone Mountain near Atlanta, Georgia, which is a granite dome of the same type as those of the Yosemite region, stands three hundred miles south of the southernmost limit reached by the continental ice sheet in the eastern part of the United States. So perfect is its similarity in shape, aspect, and even surface details that one might believe Stone Mountain had been bodily transplanted from the Sierra Nevada. Clearly, then, the rounded forms of the domes are not to be attributed to the grinding action of overriding ice.

Geologists now generally recognize that the domes owe their rounded forms to the exfoliation of massive granite—the casting off of successive curving shells or scales from their exposed surfaces. Every dome bears a number of curving shells, arranged concentrically like the layers of an onion; the outer ones break up in the course of time and drop off. On Sentinel Dome, which is readily accessible, the concentric shell structure may be studied at close hand. The shells vary from about half a foot to several feet in thickness. The outer shells are usually the thinnest. On Half Dome some of the shells are 6 to 10 feet thick; in the Royal Arches, shells measuring 10 to more than 100 feet in thickness are displayed, but these massive shells are exceptional. The total thickness of all the shells on a dome varies widely, but it seldom exceeds 100 feet. All the domes in the Yosemite region have the same structure. The shadows cast by the sharp edges of the broken shells are often so conspicuous that at a distance they look like cracks in the domes.

Comparison of this concentric dome structure to that of an onion is only partly appropriate, for the former structure penetrates as a rule but a short distance into the body of the dome and dies out toward the interior, where there is a solid core. This fact is most clearly manifest in Half Dome. As seen from North Dome, the shells terminating at its precipitous front seem little more than thin, superficial peels; the whole structure appears only "skin deep." Actually, the shells total about 100 feet in thickness, but this is insignificant in comparison with the enormous size of the rock mass, which is 2,000 feet high, 2,000 feet wide, and nearly a mile long.

But what of this colossal inner rock mass? Is it wholly structureless? Half Dome, except for the shells on its crown, is one solid, undivided block, a single gigantic monolith. And the same is true of every granite dome.

The huge, undivided lumps that constitute the domes have not always been fissureless. Close scrutiny reveals that they are traversed by what are popularly termed veins. These veins, more properly speaking, dikes, outline former joints that have been sealed again by molten material (commonly aplite, a fine-grained, cream-colored variety of granite) that was injected into them from below. The presence of two or more systems of dikes, one crossing the other, indicates several successive epochs of fracturing and sealing.

The back of Half Dome is crisscrossed by a network of crooked dikes of aplite which, owing to their greater resistance to the weather, now stand out in relief, and under a slanting light actually cast shadows, like the swollen veins on the back of one's hand. El Capitan's grand façade reveals a huge, ragged body of bluish diorite that fills an irregularly branching fracture system, and simulates in outline the map of North America—a wall map 2,000 feet high. Across this intruded mass of diorite and the surrounding granite run thin, straight dikes of yellow aplite, indicating lesser fractures of a later date. But, however badly fractured the bodies of Half Dome and El Capitan may have been in the past, today they certainly act as single, undivided blocks, and the partings between their curving surface shells cut impartially through granite, diorite, and aplite.

If every dome bears shells, has a curving surface, and is internally solid, the conclusion is unavoidable that these three phenomena are intimately associated and interrelated. Every large mass of undivided granite in the Yosemite region, whether it forms a summit or is part of a canyon wall or floor, has a tendency to cast off shells and acquire a rounded surface. Indeed, throughout the adjoining High Sierra as well, surface shells and rounded surfaces are found wherever large masses of undivided rock are exposed to view.

The cause of exfoliation is still somewhat of a mystery. That the shells burst loose from the core of a dome because of expansive stresses in the granite is clear from the facts of observation as well as from the principles of mechanics, but how the expansive stresses originate is a matter of doubt. External heating of the rock by the rays of the sun is unquestionably a factor, for on Stone Mountain, Georgia, the quarrymen, who produce shells as much as an acre in extent artificially, by blasting and pneumatic pressure, find that the process is effective only in summer, when the rock is warmed by the sun. But neither solar nor seasonal warming nor the two combined are found, upon mathematical analysis, to be capable of producing stresses powerful enough to disrupt granite to depths of as much as 100 feet. Neither can the swelling of the granite as a result of hydration—that is, the chemical union of water with the constituent minerals—be a competent cause. It can be only a feeble subsidiary cause at most, for microscopic examinations of rocks taken from some of the outermost and oldest shells of exfoliating bodies of granite reveal only signs of very moderate hydration.

The explanation probably nearest the truth is that the granite, crystallized at great depth under the pressure of thousands of feet of superincumbent rock, is now gradually expanding, being relieved from the load by erosion through millions of years. In jointed rocks such expansion is taken up by adjustments along numerous partings, but in a monolith the stresses accumulate until they exceed the tensile strength of the rock, and the outer and more rapidly expanding layer bursts loose. In the course of time the process is repeated, and the monolith becomes covered with several layers of shells. The outermost layer, being exposed to the weather, gradually disintegrates, and the pieces fall off.

Whatever the ultimate cause of exfoliation, the manner in which the process operates to produce smoothly rounded forms is clear from numerous examples. Its tendency is to eliminate projecting corners and angles and to replace them by fairly sharp curves. (See fig. 10.) With the dropping off of succeeding shells these sharp curves are replaced by more and more gentle curves, and thus a smoothly rounded surface is finally evolved.

A striking illustration of the successive steps in the process is afforded at the brink of the great precipice of Upper Yosemite Fall, near the top of the Lost Arrow. Doubtless there was originally a square edge, produced by the dropping away of the huge sheet of rock of which the Lost Arrow is the principal remnant; but in the course of the several hundred thousand years that have elapsed since the El Portal glaciation (the later ice did not touch the cliff) the square edge has been transformed by progressive exfoliation to a gently curving one. At one place, however, remains part of what was presumably the second shell to be formed, characterized by a sharply curving outer surface. The next shell under it is more gently curved, and the next more gently still.

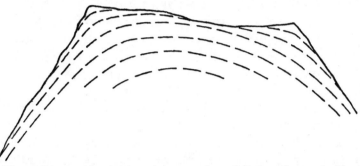

Fig. 10. Diagram showing how, by progressive exfoliation, the angularities of a rock mass are replaced by smooth curves.

Similar, but on a larger scale, is the exfoliation displayed at the edges of the Quarter Domes. These two domes owe their peculiar configuration to the controlling influence on the side facing Tenaya Canyon of northeast- and northwest-trending master joints intersecting at right angles. The domes doubtless had, at the end of the El Portal glaciation, fairly sharp points and angular edges, but exfoliation has blunted and rounded them off. On the lower Quarter Dome a sufficient number of older shells remain in place to give some indication of the original point and edges.

In both of the foregoing examples the exfoliation developed since the El Portal glaciation. The approximate length of time involved is therefore known, and thus some idea may be had of the rate at which exfoliation shells are formed. In each instance a period of several hundred thousand years was required for the moderate rounding off by exfoliation of an originally angular edge. The postglacial interval was too short, in many places, for the production of a single shell. The crown and back of Mount Broderick, which were stripped of all their shells by the overriding Merced Glacier of the Wisconsin stage, still show no signs of renewed exfoliation over the greater part of their surfaces. The severely glaciated sides of the Little Yosemite likewise are devoid of shells over large areas. Only a few thin shells have recently been detached.

It is evident that the domes of the Yosemite region have been a long time in the making; they are among the oldest features of its landscape. Their sweeping curves attest their great antiquity. Sentinel Dome and Mount Starr King, which stand above the general level of the Yosemite upland, doubtless were in process of exfoliation as far back as the Miocene epoch, at least 12,000,000 years ago, when the upland was still an undulating lowland and the Merced River flowed in a broad, shallow valley. Their evolution to the present forms may be traced through the reconstructed landscapes shown in plates 2 to 7.

The total bulk of shells cast off by each dome in that vast span of time must have been considerable; evidently the present domes are the much reduced, rounded-off remnants of originally much larger rock masses. Nevertheless, it is safe to say that all the Yosemite domes are more prominent now than ever before. It must not be forgotten that they represent the most obdurate rock masses of the region, the slowest to yield to the destructive influence of the elements. The jointed rock about them was far more vulnerable: it was fairly etched out from between the monoliths. Besides, the interval covered embraces the whole Ice Age and the preceding epoch of intense stream activity. In no other period of the same length did the Sierra Nevada suffer more rapid and profound dissection.

Some of the domes, indeed, owe their present prominence largely to the cutting of the canyons. North Dome and Basket Dome originally were inconspicuous knobs a few hundred feet above the shallow valley of Tenaya Creek. Sentinel Dome rose but a thousand feet above the path of the Merced. El Capitan and Mount Watkins, before they were undercut, were mere round-backed, sparsely forested mountain swells. And Half Dome's marvelous gain in height and majesty will be manifest when it is realized that the Little Yosemite, on its south side, was cut down 1,500 feet and Tenaya Canyon, on its north side, no less than 3,500 feet.

In spite of long-continued shelling, all the domes exhibit irregularities and eccentricities of outline: none has as yet achieved a purely hemispherical form. Each is elongated and more or less one-sided. A suggestion of their original forms remains in the present outlines. Straight sides are a common feature, and there is little doubt that the trend of these sides is inherited from master fractures that bounded the original rock masses. Dome forms grade into whaleback ridges such as Mount Watkins, Boundary Hill, and the summit of El Capitan.

Most of the domes have been derived from monoliths that had extremely irregular initial shapes. These monoliths, being surrounded by jointed granite, were bounded by fracture planes trending at various angles. The master joints of great extent gave rise to large plane surfaces.

The first shells to be formed on these plane surfaces naturally were themselves plane, or nearly so, and curved only toward the edges. They in turn transmitted their trend and angle to the next shells, and so on from shell to shell. Thus, in spite of their ever-increasing roundness of surface, the domes have continued to betray in their outline the influence of the initial bounding fracture planes.

North Dome undoubtedly owes the marked parallelism of its long, straight east and west sides to the influence of two north-northeast-trending master joints. Sentinel Dome and Mount Starr King, although they are the most perfectly shaped of the Yosemite domes, nevertheless reveal the influence of former limiting master joints with northeastward and northwestward trends. Most of the other domes also have dim facets inherited from fracture planes belonging to the northeast- and north-west-trending systems, which are the prevailing joint systems of the Yosemite region. A glance at the detailed map of Yosemite Valley will show this to be true also of Moraine Dome, the lesser domes of the Starr King group, and the domed spurs that project southwestward from them: it is most conspicuous in Basket Dome, Half Dome, Mount Broderick, and Liberty Cap.

The spurs of the Starr King group are of peculiar interest as examples of forms derived from elongated monoliths. Standing on the back of such a spur, you might imagine yourself aboard a huge whaleback steamer. Viewing them endwise, from Illilouette Valley, you might believe them to be massive, tapering rock pillars of a novel design, each wearing a close-fitting cap. Perhaps still more freakish is the cylinder-shaped ridge which advances southwestward from Indian Ridge. This ridge is surmounted by the trail to North Dome, but its true character is best appreciated from a distance, and the best view is from the summit of North Dome.

The extreme one-sidedness of Basket Dome (which, by the way, is not in the least apparent from the floor of the valley) is due to the presence on its steep northeast side of a vertical master fracture of the northwesterly system and to the absence on its gentle southwest side of any accentuated fractures. The asymmetry thus foreordained by the structure of the rock has been greatly enhanced by the undercutting action of the Tenaya Glacier, which for long periods impinged upon the sheer northeastern face, but did not rise high enough (except during the highest ice flood) to sweep away the shells from the top and the southwestern slope. Basket Dome now presents an almost grotesque appearance from the north. Its smoothed northeast side actually overhangs, and its crown and southwest side are heavily encumbered with disintegrating shells that have lain there unmolested for tens of thousands of years. A profile view shows that the dome is parted from the mountain behind it by a master fracture that dips steeply under its body and promises to give rise to additional oddities of figure.

None of the Yosemite domes reveals in its outlines the controlling influence of bounding fracture planes with more startling clearness than Half Dome. Its 2,000-foot sheer, wall-like front, the most astounding rock face in the Sierra Nevada, was obviously produced by a great master fracture. This is so patent and so strikingly impressive that tourists invariably want to know what became of the "other half" of the dome. The rounding back of the dome evokes small interest. Its curving outline seems quite normal; also, it is turned away from the valley and is relatively little known.

It is not generally appreciated that the great back, though gently rounded, is on the whole parallel to the sheer front. Both back and front appear to have inherited their trends from northeasterly master fractures. Why, then, do they differ signally in form and character? The sheer front is essentially plane and looks as if it had been cleft through the body of the dome. It does, indeed, suggest what J. Smeaton Chase refers to as "a frightful amputation," which left sharp edges and even undercut the shells on the crown so that they now hang over like the eaves of a roof. The back, on the contrary, curves without break into the crown and sides, its huge, wonderfully continuous shells wrapping around these parts. How could fractures similar in trend and attitude have given rise to surfaces wholly dissimilar in modeling?

The difference between the front and the back of the dome is primarily a difference in age: the rounded back is a very ancient feature; the sheer front is a relatively modern one. The back of Half Dome, like the crown and sides, has been casting off shells for ages—ever since the Little Yosemite began to be carved by the Merced in Tertiary time. Its northeastward trend and prevailing flatness are merely inheritances from a structure now extinct. But the sheer front still has the freshness of youth; it was made only yesterday, geologically speaking.

On the north side of Half Dome the rock was not massive and undivided like that of the monolith itself, but was sliced by parallel, steeply dipping fractures, having a declivity of 82°, into a multitude of thin, standing sheets trending toward the northeast. This sheeted structure terminated in the shoulder at the northeastern end of the cliff face, and it has given rise to a sharply incised notch at the southwestern end. Water percolating through the fissures and freezing in them wrought havoc among the sheets and in time converted the northern slope into a ruinous jumble of slabs and slivers.

Then came the Ice Age, and the Tenaya Glacier, which during the earlier stages of glaciation came within 500 feet of the top of the dome, in driving against the rock mass swept away the debris and tore off fresh rock sheets. The receding glacier left a steep-walled recess in which snow-banks lingered far into the summer. Aided by their chilling presence, the frost carried on the work of destruction until all the rock sheets were gone except a few stubs that remain to attest the character of the de-molished structure.

Now that the body of the great monolith stands uncovered—it has been so probably most of the time since the El Portal stage of glaciation—the monolith has begun to produce shells by exfoliating in plane sheets parallel to the zone of joints. The process has not yet gone very far, but the rock face reveals a faint yet unmistakable curvature of the surface toward the edges. At the top, especially, the curvature is pronounced, and there considerable masses of incurving shells have recently dropped away, leaving a dangerously overhanging cornice of older, top shells—the well-known "vizor" of the dome.

This interpretation of the evolution of Half Dome precludes any assumed demolition of one-half of the dome. No such assumption appears justified by the facts known about the structure of the rock on the north-west side of Half Dome, nor would it accord with the present conception of the erosional origin of Yosemite Valley and Tenaya Canyon. Had there been another half of the dome consisting of a gigantic monolith, it would still be in existence, for neither the glacier nor the agents of normal erosion that shaped the preglacial valley of Tenaya Creek could have demolished it.

The curving back of Half Dome is evidently a product of long-continued exfoliation. Shells have been forming on it and dropping from it for millions of years. The slowness of the process may be judged from the fact that the huge shell that envelops almost the entire back of the dome has been in place so long that furrows several feet deep have been worn in it by the rock grains washed from the crown. The central parts of the shell have so many furrows that they present a ribbed or fluted appearance.

On the broad crown of Half Dome, where gravity and snowslides are not effective removing agents, the shells remain in place still longer. They remain, in fact, until they disintegrate into mere slivers and grains of rock, mainly as a result of daily heating by the sun, in less measure because of recurrent frost action. Thus the dome bears on its summit a great accumulation of old shells, the aggregate thickness being estimated at 90 to 100 feet.

Half Dome is not the only dome of the Yosemite region that bears lineaments of recent origin. Some domes may well be described as altogether "new" to the Yosemite landscape, having been sculptured by the ice. Liberty Cap, Mount Broderick, and Sugar Loaf are obdurate monoliths that have remained standing in the path of the Merced Glacier while the surrounding, jointed granite was quarried and swept away by the ice.

Before the Ice Age, Liberty Cap and Mount Broderick were merely knobs on a continuous, hummocky ridge or spur that projected southward from the base of Half Dome. The overriding ice singled out the weakest spot in the ridge, a narrow zone traversed by northeast-trending fractures, and gouged out the slivered rock to produce the accentuated V cleft that now separates Liberty Cap from Mount Broderick. The opposing flanks of the two monoliths, although somewhat rounded by the ice, still outline with fidelity the shape of the slivered rock mass that formerly lay between them. Their outer flanks also reflect in their trends the influence of the northeasterly fractures that formerly adjoined them. The backs of both domes have been rounded by the grinding ice so that their former angularities have been greatly dimmed, though not wholly effaced. But the fronts, having been subjected to glacial quarrying rather than grinding, are still conspicuously angular and reveal in their trends and alignment the influence of northwest-trending fractures.

Of all the newer domes, Sugar Loaf alone exhibits no marked angularities or facets. Probably it was enveloped on all sides, except on the north side, which is attached to the wall of the Little Yosemite, by more or less rhythmically divided rock that was worn away with almost equal readiness on every hand, and so it was rounded to its present strikingly symmetrical figure.

A rare type of sculpture produced characteristically in exfoliating granite and associated with the domes consists of successive arches recessed one within another. The back of Half Dome is an imperfect example, yet it shows clearly how such arches originate through the caving off of the lower portions of shells. The remaining portion of each shell tends to assume the shape of an arch, which as architects well know, is the form of structure best adapted to bear a heavy, distributed load.

The finest example is afforded by the Royal Arches. They are fashioned on a colossal scale, the main arch rising to a height of 1,000 feet (measured to its underside) and having a span of 1,800 feet.[1] Many shells are from 10 to 80 feet thick, and several of them unite near the top of the main arch to form one shell nearly 200 feet thick. The Yosemite Glacier was

---

[1] The Royal Arches remind one of the recessed semicircular arches over the doorways of some of the mediaeval cathedrals of France and Great Britain (notably Avallon, Caen, and Canterbury). Such arches form a particularly durable type of structure, and are relatively easy to erect, the central arch being of small span and giving support to the larger arches above it.

the principal sculptor; during the latest stage of glaciation it plucked away the lower portions of the shells, which had previously been loosened by exfoliation from a partial, low-set dome that bulged into the valley. The great strength of the massive shells has permitted the forming of exceptionally high and broad arches, and the homogeneity of the granite has given rise to unusually perfect, smooth curvature. A short distance west of the Royal Arches is another set of arches, sculptured likewise by the Yosemite Glacier but from much thinner shells. Because of their proximity to the Royal Arches they receive little attention, yet they are a good average example of the type as it occurs in different parts of the Sierra Nevada.

The shells produced by exfoliation are not all convexly curved. On the cliff face of Half Dome they are plane, and the same is true elsewhere, notably on the south side of the Little Yosemite. There are, however, also examples of concave exfoliation, the shells produced having hollow outer surfaces. Wherever a powerful glacier, after plucking away all the exfoliation shells, gouges a structureless mass of granite in the bottom or side of its channel, it tends to grind out a smoothly concave surface. When exfoliation begins anew, it produces concave shells.

Imperfect examples of concave shells are to be seen in the salient of El Capitan, which is itself an imperfect dome, not wholly massive throughout, that has been vigorously gouged by the Yosemite Glacier. Much finer examples of concave exfoliation are afforded by Mount Watkins, the southeast side of which was gouged by the Tenaya Glacier and by the shallow glacial cirques that scallop the great cliff front of Clouds Rest. Concave exfoliation on a large scale is exhibited in the canyon of the Merced River above Vernal Fall. The sides and floor of that canyon exfoliate in more or less concave shells parallel to its U-shaped cross profile. Emerald Pool occupies the central basin gouged by the Merced Glacier in massive granite. Many similar examples of glacial U canyons and cirques with walls and floors exfoliating in concave curves exist in the High Sierra above the Yosemite region. It is not to be supposed that these canyons and cirques were excavated in rock that was traversed originally by concentric U partings; on the contrary, the partings have been developed since the canyons and cirques were gouged.

If the last episode in the evolution of the Yosemite—that of glacial excavating—brought into prominence many domes that were before inconspicuous, and even uncovered several new bosses, is it not to be expected that further deepening, whether by moving ice or by running water, will give birth to other domes? Such further deepening is certain to ensue. The Merced River, descending through the Yosemite region with a gradient averaging 250 feet to the mile, is capable of cutting into the granite at least another thousand feet and has already entered upon the task. Its side streams are slowly deepening their valleys and gulches, and dissecting the uplands that border the chasm.

The Yosemite's cliffs and the adjoining uplands reveal an abundance of material for the making of new domes. Every one of the many rounded, half-bare swells of the upland surface betrays the presence of a great monolith that need only be unearthed to become a dome. So do the massive, unfissured bodies of granite in the walls of the chasm, already conspicuous because of their barrenness.

The enormous, billowy terraces of granite that flank the Merced Canyon above the Little Yosemite will at some time not far distant, geologically speaking, resolve themselves into a great herd of domes. The two promontories of Cascade Cliffs, in the Little Yosemite, are well on the way toward being detached and transformed into domes. But other masses lie still so far beneath the general level of the land that millions of years must pass before they can become surface features. Such are the huge monoliths that form the basement of Clouds Rest and the pedestal of Half Dome. But the most noteworthy and most colossal of these deep-seated masses is that which slopes down in a smoothly rounded, spreading cone beneath the cliffs of Glacier Point. At least 1,500 feet high, as far as it is exposed to view, and more than half a mile in diameter, it bids fair, in another geologic period, to become an enormous and exceptionally beautiful dome, a worthy successor to Half Dome and its peers.

7

The marks of time

It remains to consider the changes wrought in Yosemite Valley during the relatively few thousands of years that have elapsed since the end of the Ice Age. The magnitude of those changes is commonly underestimated. Indeed, the belief seems to prevail that the Yosemite region presents today much the same appearance as it did immediately after the evacuation of the ice. However, postglacial time, though brief in the geologic sense, has sufficed to permit disintegration, erosion, and deposition to accomplish significant results. The valley walls have been partially dismantled and cloaked with rock waste at their bases; and the lake basins excavated by the glaciers have been filled with stream-borne sediments. The Yosemite region has therefore lost much of its ice-given grandeur and grimness of aspect and has gained in habitableness and charm.

The most radical changes produced in the landscape will be described first: those due to the complete obliteration of the glacial lakes. The camper who pitches his tent in one of the Yosemite's shady groves may not realize that the spot once lay in the midst of a mountain lake of exceptional beauty, in which the cliffs of El Capitan and Half Dome as well as the sprays of the Yosemite Falls were reflected.

Ancient Lake Yosemite occupied the entire length and breadth of the main Yosemite chamber. It was five and a half miles long, extending from the moraine dam at El Capitan Bridge to the great wall at the head of the valley, and its waters lapped the bases of the freshly glaciated walls on each side. The lake owed its existence not to the morainal dam alone; it occupied an elongated basin scooped in the rock floor of the valley by the ancient Yosemite Glacier, and its depth was merely increased somewhat by the moraine dam, which was situated on a broad rock sill at the lower end of the basin.

The depth of the lake basin is not known, as no borings have ever been made, but cross profiles of the valley, plotted accurately from the contouring of the topographic map, give a fair basis for estimates. If the bottom curves in these profiles are drawn in accordance with the characteristics of the exposed rock floors of other Yosemite-like canyons in the High Sierra, they indicate depths ranging from 100 feet to not less than 300 feet. The basin was probably deepest in the upper part of the valley, opposite Yosemite Village.[1]

The filling of the lake no doubt began before the ice completely left the valley, but the main work was done by the Merced River and Tenaya Creek. When the Yosemite Glacier had departed, these streams began to deposit glacial debris. The resulting deltas in time coalesced into one large delta when the streams joined. This large delta then grew forward down the valley until, probably in the course of thousands of years, its front reached the moraine dam, and the basin was completely filled.

The appearance of Lake Yosemite during its gradual extinction and the aspect of the delta at its head may be readily imagined by anyone who has visited Merced Lake or Washburn Lake. Each of these lakes is now being encroached upon, in the same manner, by a slowly forward-growing delta composed of stream-borne sand and gravel. Each lake, in fact, is already reduced to two-thirds its original length and has at its head a delta plain half a mile long. These delta plains have gently sloping surfaces, cut only by the channel of the river and by a few old, abandoned channels.

It is probable that, like the deltas at Merced Lake and Washburn

---

[1] On the basis of geophysical studies made in 1934 and 1935, Dr. B. Gutenberg and Dr. J. P. Buwalda have assigned depths of considerably greater magnitude to the fill in Yosemite Valley; the maximum depths indicated by their data occur between the Government Administration Building and Camp Curry. See John P. Buwalda, "Form and Depth of the Bedrock Trough of Yosemite Valley," *Yosemite Nature Notes*, October, 1941, pp. 89–93.

Lake, the delta at the head of Lake Yosemite was largely covered with vegetation. Its more stable portions bore forest trees, and its shore was fringed with willows. That the climatic conditions permitted vegetation to establish itself upon the delta soon after the retreat of the glaciers can scarcely be doubted, for there are indications in various parts of the Sierra Nevada that even during glacial time extensive forests of pine and sequoia flourished on its lower slope and well up on the ridges between the canyons.

As the delta plain was extended forward it was also built up gradually, for the streams, which were heavily loaded with debris, had to maintain a sufficient slope to transport it. The coarser material they dropped soon after emerging into the valley; thus their gradients were steepest at the valley head. They had a fall there of about 20 feet to the mile, whereas throughout the greater part of the lake basin they had a fall of only 3 feet to the mile.

The present valley floor does not represent the original delta plain that was formed in the manner just described, but is a relatively new plain that lies 14 to 16 feet lower. Probably as the result of a rather sudden breaching of the moraine dam the Merced River cut down its bed and trenched the plain until at length it established a new grade similar to the first. Then, winding sluggishly from side to side, it widened out a new plain at the expense of the old one. In only a few places are remnants of the old plain left, in the form of terraces. A particularly prominent terrace of this sort overlooks Tenaya Creek near the head of the valley. The level plain in front of Camp Curry is another terrace. More extensive remnants of the old plain occur north of the Cathedral Spires and the Cathedral Rocks.

The present valley floor has the characteristic features of what is properly termed a flood plain: low natural levees along the riverbanks slope gently away from the stream and are breached in places by overflow channels, and in the plain beyond are numerous crescent-shaped sloughs outlining old oxbow bends abandoned by the river when it shifted its course. These are all evidences that the river has almost ceased to cut, and at times of high water builds up the valley somewhat by depositing sediment. Every year, usually in May, floodings occur as a result of the rapid melting of snow in the High Sierra. Fortunately, the water spreads only over the lower ground and attains a depth of only a few feet. No material damage is done, as all permanent structures in the valley are built on relatively high ground.

The Little Yosemite once contained a lake that must have extended over the entire length and breadth of the floor, measuring about two and a half miles long and somewhat less than half a mile wide. Like the body of water in Yosemite Valley, it lay in a rock basin scooped out by the glaciers, but it was impounded only by a rock barrier and had no moraine dam. The rock barrier at the lower end, now cleft by a narrow gorge through which the river passes in brawling rapids, is about half a mile above Nevada Fall. The lake shallowed gradually toward its outlet and probably attained no great depth at any point. The deposit of river gravel that now fills the basin is not thick enough to cover the crests of the numerous small moraines which the retreating Merced Glacier left behind. Some of these moraines cross the basin fully a mile above the outlet. They stood probably only about 30 feet high; hence the depth of the lake in that vicinity must have been only about 25 feet. The maximum depth occurred probably half a mile farther up and may have exceeded 50 feet.

A basin so shallow was not long in filling. The lake in the Little Yosemite, therefore, was obliterated perhaps even before Lake Yosemite was filled, although the Little Yosemite was evacuated by the ice much later than the main valley. The general process of filling, by the forward growth of a delta, no doubt was the same in each lake.

Lost Lake has probably always been a separate body of water, not communicating with the larger lake in the Little Yosemite. It lies on a rock bench raised somewhat above the river gravel in the Little Yosemite and is walled in on the southeast side by a moraine. It owes its existence to the collection of seepage water and the runoff from the surrounding mountain sides. Lost Lake is now being filled gradually with a deposit of peat resulting from the accumulation of vegetal material. It is little more than a watery swamp and will soon reach the stage when it can no longer be referred to as a lake.

It may seem anomalous that Emerald Pool, the smallest of all the glacial lakes in the Yosemite region, should still be unfilled and in precisely the same condition as at the end of the glacial epoch. The explanation is found in the very smallness of the basin, in the smoothness of its sides and bottom, which are composed of massive granite throughout, and in the great momentum with which the Merced River rushes into the pool as a result of its descent in the Silver Apron. At times of flood, all the water in the pool is set in motion and the powerful current sweeps through it unchecked, carrying sand and gravel with it.

Although the steps in the floor of Tenaya Canyon are not especially clean-cut, their configuration indicates or at least suggests the former existence of a glacially scooped lake basin on each tread. There were apparently four such lake basins in the stretch extending from the mouth of the canyon to the great step from which Tenaya Cascade descends. The upper three were little more than ponds that must have been quickly filled, but the lowermost, near the mouth of the canyon, was over a mile in length and probably was not filled until a long time after the glacier had withdrawn from the canyon.

Mirror Lake might readily be supposed to be a remnant of this ancient lake—in fact, it is often assumed to be of glacial origin, like most lakes in the High Sierra—but actually it is of relatively recent making and had no connection with the Ice Age. It is impounded wholly by masses of rock debris that fell in avalanches from both walls of the canyon, principally from a place on the west wall just back of the Washington Column. (See p. 139.) West of the outlet of the lake, it is true, there is a small quantity of morainal debris, readily distinguishable from the angular avalanche material by its water-rounded and glacier-polished cobbles and pebbles; but there is no dam composed of such glacial material across the canyon.

The creation of Mirror Lake by obstructing rock avalanches was of course favored by the fact that the lower part of Tenaya Canyon already had a nearly level floor, owing to the previous filling of a glacial lake basin. Had the floor not been so nearly level, the low, irregular avalanche dam would not have backed up the water for any great distance.

The relative recency of its creation explains why little Mirror Lake is still in existence, whereas the large lake basin in Yosemite Valley is completely filled. Mirror Lake itself, however, appears to be not far removed from extinction. The rate at which the delta at its head is encroaching upon it from year to year is sufficiently rapid to be discernible to the eye. Indeed, unless steps are taken to check the further growth of the delta, Mirror Lake will soon be reduced to a small, unimpressive pond, and the Yosemite region will lose one of its most valued scenic treasures.

Because of the sheerness of its walls, Yosemite Valley has been the scene of many rock falls. The glaciers, having transformed it from a V-shaped canyon to a U-shaped trough, left the Yosemite at the end of the Ice Age with oversteepened sides—that is, with cliffs more precipitous than weathering and erosion would have produced. When these processes again prevailed, upon the departure of the glaciers, the cliffs tended to revert to less bold and more stable forms.

This dismantling has made little progress, and most of the cliffs still retain their glacial profiles. The extent of the damage they have suffered is most readily estimated from the size of the piles of rock waste that lie at their bases. These piles, or taluses, are for the most part small—surprisingly small in comparison with the long slopes of rock waste that partly cloak the sides of the glaciated valleys in the Rocky Mountains, the Cascade Range, and the Alps. So insignificant do they seem under the imposing rock façades of Yosemite Valley that many observers have commented on the apparent absence of debris. In reality, however, there is hardly a spot at the base of the cliffs where rock waste is entirely absent. Only in a few places are there piles less than 50 feet high. At the toe of El Capitan, which has the appearance of rising directly from the valley floor, there are fully 100 feet of debris. Under most of the great cliffs the debris attains heights of 250 to 500 feet; in a few recesses it reaches 2,000 feet.

What has been said thus far, however, applies strictly to the upper Yosemite chamber. The lower chamber is, by contrast, fairly lined with rock waste. The taluses slope out so far from each side as to leave but a narrow strip of valley bottom free. The Rock Slides across which the Big Oak Flat Road is graded are two miles broad and reach almost to the brink of the upland. This marked difference in the amount of rock waste in the upper and lower chambers is explained by the fact that in the upper chamber rock waste has accumulated only since the last glaciation, that is, for a relatively few thousands of years. In the lower chamber, where the last Yosemite glacier did not penetrate, it has been accumulating ever since the earlier or El Portal glaciation, that is, for a period of several hundred thousand years. But there also is the fact that the walls of the upper chamber are composed of prevailingly massive or sparsely jointed rocks, whereas the walls of the lower chamber are composed in large part of well-jointed rocks. Its north wall, which consists mostly of closely fractured gabbro, has suffered the most complete demolition. Only a few crags of it remain standing above the vast rock talus.

The spacing of the joint fractures in the rocks, which was a potent factor in determining the rate of glacial excavation, has also controlled the rate of postglacial dismantling. Where joints are most numerous and closely spaced, the dismantling has proceeded most rapidly; where joints are few and far apart, the dismantling has been correspondingly slow. Throughout the Yosemite region, the size of the debris piles and the joint structure of the cliffs above them are closely related. The upper Yosemite chamber, especially, offers striking variations. At the extreme point of the Cathedral Rocks, where the granite is particularly massive, there are scarcely 50 feet of debris, but in the recesses adjoining the Cathedral Spires, where shattered diorite and gabbro prevail, the debris reaches a height of 2,000 feet. East of Taft Point, where the cliffs are more sparingly fractured, the debris again dwindles to a mere 100 feet. The sheeted granodiorite in and about Sentinel Rock has given rise to taluses 600 to 1,500 feet in height, but the relatively massive granite which alternates with the granodiorite in the cliffs under Union Point has produced a talus only 50 feet high. On the north side of the valley, likewise, the debris piles vary from 100 feet at the base of the Three Brothers to 1,100 feet in the embayment to the east, where they afford a convenient slope for the zigzag trail to Yosemite Falls. Under Columbia Rock, on the other hand, there is less than 50 feet of debris. In general, each embayment or recess that marks a place of weakness in the walls of the valley contains a great cone of debris; each promontory that marks a point of strength has a minimum of debris at its base.

The belief prevails among visitors to Yosemite Valley that most of the rock debris was thrown down from the cliffs by earthquakes, for some of the boulders are astonishingly large and lie far out in the valley. Then, too, the walls are so massive that nothing less than an earthquake would seem sufficient to break them down. Nor is there lacking observational evidence of the efficacy with which earthquakes can disrupt the walls and produce rock debris. John Muir was privileged to witness the rare spectacle of the downfall of a pinnacle—Eagle Rock, on the south wall of the valley not far from Moran Point—at the time of the Owens Valley earthquake in 1872. He has left us a graphic account of the great avalanche of bounding rock fragments that resulted from the crash.

A considerable part of the rock waste in Yosemite Valley may be of earthquake origin, for tremors must have occurred during the postglacial interval as a result of minor movements along the fault fractures at the eastern base of the range (pp. 44–47). It is fairly certain that at least one strong shock was felt in Yosemite Valley, for only thirty miles away, near the western shore of Mono Lake, the moraines at the mouth of Lundy Canyon are cut across by a fault scarp 50 feet high that was probably produced by a single, sudden earth movement.

But whether most of the rock waste in the Yosemite Valley is to be accredited to one strong quake, or even to all the postglacial quakes together, seems doubtful. Rock waste is being shed from the cliffs in quantities at the present time, as a result of normal weathering and disintegration and the recurrent action of snow avalanches and torrential rains; this intermittent shedding of debris doubtless has gone on ever since the glaciers vanished. To credit earthquakes with perhaps half of the total amount of rock waste in the valley, therefore, would probably be liberal.

Significant light was shed on this question some years ago, when an excavation for road material was begun at the toe of the great rock talus under the Big Oak Flat Road. In the head wall of this excavation were visible no less than four distinct layers of rock debris, each several feet in thickness and separated from the next by a thin layer of dark, earthy matter of vegetal origin, doubtless ancient soil. Roots and stumps of forest trees were embedded in these soils. It was thus made clear that this talus had been formed not by a single huge avalanche, but by successive avalanches that were separated by long intervals during each of which a forest was able to establish itself upon the slope.

Whether the avalanches were thrown down by earthquakes it is impossible to say. Some may have fallen without such action. A cliff that has long stood essentially unchanged in outer appearance often becomes so weakened internally by the solvent action of acid-bearing waters percolating through the joint cracks that its component parts lose coherence and crash under the pull of gravity alone. An occurrence of this kind was observed near the base of the Three Brothers in 1923. A large sheet or spall of rock suddenly detached itself from the cliff face without being impelled by any noticeable earth tremor and, as it fell, crushed and obliterated with its debris a forest of pine trees that had grown on the talus below. Spontaneous rock falls of this sort probably account for a large share of the vast talus over which the Big Oak Flat Road is laid and likewise of other taluses in the valley.

The visitor need have little fear that spontaneous rock avalanches will occur while he is in Yosemite Valley, for such avalanches are infrequent in a valley the walls of which are so massive. Only in the few spots where the rock is shattered into small fragments and ground water is fairly abundant are rock falls likely to occur annually or at shorter intervals, for there alternating frost and thaw, heat and cold, are effective agents. In those places, which are for the most part in recesses, the talus has a relatively fresh appearance and is either bare or scantily covered with bushes.

Most of the minor rock falls in the Yosemite region take place in winter or in spring, in conjunction with snow avalanches or in thawing weather. On the steep northwestern slope of Clouds Rest, snow avalanches are the principal agency and have worn smooth, funnel-shaped tracks. During the long, dry summers, rock falls are rare but not wholly absent. Tenaya Canyon has a particularly evil reputation in this regard. The few mountaineers who have had the hardihood to traverse this canyon appear to have been as much impressed by the peril of falling rocks as by the unusual obstacles to climbing.

An agency which is effective in causing the mechanical disruption of the granitic rocks in the Yosemite region is the radiant heat of the sun. Several circumstances operate to intensify its action. The absence of vegetation and even of soil exposes the rock over large areas to the rays of the sun. Because of the dryness and purity of the air, together with its thinness at high altitudes, the rays suffer relatively little loss of heat through absorption or reflection by particles of water vapor and dust.

And the cloudless skies that prevail in summer permit them to strike the rock unhindered day after day, often for weeks or months at a stretch. Thus the rock is subjected to prolonged periods of intense daily insolation alternating with rapid cooling through irradiation at night.

All granitic rocks are aggregates of several different minerals—mainly feldspar, quartz, mica, and hornblende—the crystals of which are tightly interlocked. When these crystals expand upon being heated they tend to wedge and pry one another apart. A few heatings have no effect, but thousands upon thousands of heatings gradually loosen the crystals until

Fig. 11. Section across parts of Moraine Dome showing the features on and near its summit that afford a measure of the stripping effected since the earlier glaciation. *A* is the 7-foot wall consisting of the exposed upper part of a vertical dike of aplite; *B* is the dethroned boulder leaning against its pedestal; *C* is the 8-foot wall produced by an inclined dike of aplite. The features are shown in their true proportions, but closer together than they actually are. The broken line *G–G* indicates approximately the original ice-smoothed surface of the dome; the arrows show the direction in which the glacier moved.

they are detached in flakes or individually. In roaming through the Sierra Nevada one sometimes finds rock fragments which, although apparently solid, cannot be picked up entire, but break up into loose grains that run through the fingers like coarse sand. "Rotten" fragments of this kind occur only where the heat of the sun is felt daily.

The summits of domes that were not overridden by the glaciers of the Ice Age, such as Sentinel Dome and Half Dome, and the summits of domes that were overridden by the earlier glaciers only, such as North Dome, Basket Dome, the Quarter Domes, and Moraine Dome, afford particularly good places to observe the disruptive effect of solar heat on granite. The granite there is characteristically flaky parallel to the surface; the outer, more intensely heated layers have evidently tended to burst loose by expansion from the less intensely heated layers underneath. (The production of curving shells, one to several feet thick, by exfoliation involves agencies other than solar heat, and is not to be confounded with the flaking here discussed.) The flakes break up into individual rock grains, which eventually are washed away by the rain water. The great accumulations of granite sand in the vicinity of domes and other bare masses of granite are produced largely in this way. Frost presumably plays a part in this mechanical disruption, but a very subordinate one, for typical frost cracks are absent in the domes and other rock masses.

It is a highly significant fact that the loose grains derived from disintegrating granite in the Yosemite region show scarcely any effects of chemical decomposition. The crystals of feldspar are but slightly cloudy at the edges, and the flakes of biotite and rods of hornblende usually show no alteration. This is very different from the conditions prevailing in the eastern part of the United States and other regions of fairly high humidity, where granitic rocks are reduced by chemical decomposition into clayey soils. However, this crumbling of granite into undecomposed grains takes place only on domes, cliffs, and other conspicuously bare rock masses in the Yosemite region that are subjected to intense insolation. In densely forested areas on the uplands, where the heat of the sun is partly excluded by foliage and where the granite is covered by a layer of moisture-conserving, acid-producing humus, the chemical processes reduce the granite in much the same way as in a humid region.

A few of the outstanding evidences of earthquake action may be pointed out. Most spectacular among these are the gigantic blocks commonly referred to as earthquake boulders. A few isolated blocks near LeConte Memorial Lodge are as large as cabins and seldom fail to attract the attention of the passer-by. Blocks of various size are interspersed among the houses in the old Yosemite Village, which was built at the toe of a chaotic pile of rock debris. Blocks encumber the channel of the Merced River in the gorge below the valley, causing the stream to dash itself into foam in its wild descent; these are not boulders rolled down by the current but blocks that have fallen from the walls of the gorge. Most remarkable of all is the famous Arch Rock; between and under its enormous overarching fragments the automobile road passes about three miles above El Portal.

Though earthquake shocks undeniably afford the most plausible explanation for the dislodgment of these huge blocks, it must be admitted that there is no clear, uncontrovertible proof. Any or all of the blocks could have been dislodged without the aid of an earthquake, simply as the result of the normal weathering and disintegration of the cliffs. For in many places along the Yosemite's walls, owing to irregularities in the joint structure, very large blocks are flanked or underlain by thin slabs or mere slivers of rock. As these small fragments are loosened and dislodged, the large blocks are left in unstable positions. Even if no earth tremors should intervene, the blocks would eventually tumble down for lack of adequate support. Nor is the great distance at which the blocks lie from the parent wall necessarily an indication of earthquake action. Any block falling from a great height is likely to bound far out, and the larger and heavier the block the greater its momentum and the farther it will bound.

The probability that the blocks are of earthquake origin is greatly increased by the fact that in the Yosemite region there are several masses of rock debris of enormous extent. These are quite distinct from the ordinary sloping taluses by reason of their irregular, hummocky, sprawling forms, which can scarcely be accounted for except by the agency of earthquakes. One of these chaotic, far-flung masses obstructs the mouth of Tenaya Canyon and impounds Mirror Lake. (See p. 133.) It was derived from the wall back of the Washington Column and met lesser avalanches that fell, presumably at the same time, from the cliffs west of Half Dome. The water that issues from Mirror Lake in part percolates through the mass of debris, as is manifest at times of low water, when the stream bed is dry for some distance.

Another far-flung mass of rock debris of the same character lies at the head of Yosemite Valley, just south of Tenaya Canyon. It is spread over a space of many acres and projects a quarter of a mile from the base of the head wall, necessitating a curve in the road south of Tenaya Creek. But the most remarkable body of earthquake debris lies in front of El Capitan—not the talus of blocks that slopes steeply from the cliff to the valley floor, but the much vaster hummocky mass, partly obscured by trees and brush, that sprawls nearly half a mile into the valley, as far as the automobile road, which makes a detour around its edge. There can be no doubt that it is the product of one colossal avalanche that came down from the whole height of the cliff face—probably the most spectacular rock avalanche that has fallen in Yosemite Valley since the glacial epoch.

The sweeping concave lines of El Capitan's great façade are usually regarded as characteristic products of glacial erosion that have suffered scarcely any change from postglacial weathering. Some observers, even, have believed that they could detect on its face the gleam of glacier polish. Yet the quantity of debris that fell in this stupendous earthquake avalanche is so great—it covers nearly a quarter of a square mile of ground to an estimated depth of fully 100 feet—that its removal doubtless altered appreciably the contour and appearance of El Capitan.

All the great masses of debris must have fallen long ago, for they all support old and large trees. Perhaps they were precipitated by the severe earthquake that originated near Mono Lake. Apparently only moderate

quakes have occurred since then. The quake of 1872 was probably one
of the strongest that has taken place in historic times. No tremors of
consequence have since made themselves felt in Yosemite Valley. Indeed,
the Sierra Nevada is today a region of marked stability; this fact is strikingly attested by the presence of precariously balanced pinnacles and
rocks such as the Agassiz Column, which stands near the trail just below
Union Point.

The debris piles everywhere are subject to the washing action of rain-
water rills. As a result, they are fringed by gently sloping aprons of granite sand that spread out some distance on the floor of the valley. Where
the water is concentrated in torrents of considerable volume, however,
not merely sand grains but blocks up to 10 and even 15 feet in diameter
are washed down. These coarse materials are spread out in what are
properly termed "fans." This is true especially at the mouths of deep-cut
recesses from which the storm waters issue in short-lived torrents of incredible swiftness and power.

The most extraordinary features of the fan are the walls of blocks that
flank the diverging channels. These are not natural levees of debris, but
are really walls built of superimposed blocks. Most of them are only
3 to 5 feet high, but some are twice as high. A few contain blocks 10 to
15 feet in diameter upon which smaller fragments have been thrown by
the tumultuous waters.

The precise manner in which the channel walls are built by the torrents is not known from direct observation, but that the blocks are really
tossed up and not merely dropped by overflowing water may be inferred
from facts that were observed in 1919, a short time after unusually violent
floods had taken place in the recesses near the Cathedral Spires. The
trees near the channel walls were barked and bruised by leaping blocks
to a height of 5 to 8 feet; many new blocks had been added to the walls,
but there was no evidence of overflow on the ground behind the walls. At
the foot of each fan, where the water lost its momentum and spread out
unconfined, was a field of blocks aggregating thousands of tons in weight.
All this material had been brought down in less than half an hour, probably during one great rush of water at the climax of the flood.

The rocky platform at Glacier Point, from which the sightseer beholds
the grand panorama of Yosemite Valley and the High Sierra, presents
features that are commonly, though erroneously, regarded as evidences
of the passage of a glacier over the promontory. (Whether Glacier Point
was named for these features is uncertain. The origin of the name is
obscure.) The features mentioned are basin-shaped cavities in the rock,
measuring 12 to 18 inches in diameter, and from a few inches to 6 inches
in depth. They bear some resemblance to the potholes that are worn in

the rocky beds of streams by cobbles whirled by a swift current, especially in the deeper basins.

In the minds of many persons, such potholes are associated with glaciers, being held to be characteristic products of "glacier mills" (called *moulins* by the Swiss), that is, torrents of water descending through crevasses in the ice and impinging with great force on the rock bed below. Potholes, however, are formed by whirling cobbles in the beds of open streams as well as in the beds of subglacial streams and do not, therefore, afford prima facie evidence of glaciation. Potholes of both kinds abound in the Sierra Nevada. A fine series of potholes that are unquestionably of subglacial origin is to be seen at the lower end of Tuolumne Meadows, extending across the ice-smoothed slope of a low dome of granite where no stream could have flowed in the open. Potholes that clearly have been formed without the intervention of a glacier are plentiful in the lower Merced Canyon and in other canyons and gulches that have never been penetrated by glaciers.

The cavities at Glacier Point are not stream-worn potholes but products of strongly localized weathering, a process that affects the granitic rocks of the Sierra Nevada in many exposed places. They belong to a class of features that will here be referred to as "weather pits." The development of cavities of this type is promoted by the presence in the rock of local aggregates of readily soluble minerals. A small initial hollow is formed by the decomposition of such aggregates, and this hollow becomes a receptacle for water from rains or melting snow. The hollow is gradually enlarged by chemical and mechanical processes: acids produced by decomposing pine needles, lichens, or other vegetal matter attack the weaker minerals; and in freezing weather the ice, expanding with force as it crystallizes, pries off flakes and grains of rock. Thus weather pits may expand from a diameter of about an inch to diameters of 2 or 3 feet, and adjoining pits may eventually coalesce as their rims intersect. Their growth in depth, on the contrary, seldom keeps pace with their lateral expansion, for the less soluble particles of rock detached from the rims collect at the bottom and, although the finer particles are blown out by the wind in dry weather, usually enough of the coarser ones remain to form a protective pad that tends to retard downward excavation.

Some weather pits are difficult to distinguish from stream-worn potholes, but such pits usually possess characteristics that set them clearly apart: the processes whereby they are enlarged, being dependent mainly upon the presence of standing water, operate intensively only up to the level of the water surface and thus tend to undercut the sides, leaving the rims overhanging. This undercutting action is intensified in weather pits in which the depth of water is controlled by an outlet, giving rise to sharply overhanging rims. Some pits have alcove-like recesses under the rim, which show that enlargement is proceeding more rapidly at some points than at others. The resultant scalloped form contrasts strikingly with the smoothly cylindrical forms characteristic of true potholes produced by the grinding, boring action of whirling cobbles.

It is a significant fact that weather pits do not occur on freshly glaciated rock surfaces. Not a single one is to be found within the area that was covered by the later glaciers. Evidently they develop at an extremely slow rate, and not enough time even for their initiation has elapsed since the glacial epoch. Weather pits do occur, however, on rock surfaces that were overridden by the earlier glaciers, as well as on surfaces that have remained wholly unglaciated; the two kinds are indistinguishable so far as effects of weathering are concerned. Particularly fine examples of weather pits that have developed since the passage of the earlier ice are to be seen on the summit of North Dome; weather pits that have developed in unglaciated localities are found on the summits of Sentinel Dome and Illilouette Ridge.

The presence of weather pits on Glacier Point thus clearly affords no proof of the glaciation of that promontory, but it attests its long exposure to the weather since it was glaciated.

8 The waterfalls

However impressive are Yosemite's cliffs and monuments, the valley is famed chiefly for its waterfalls. The tumultuous descent of foam-white water from great heights is a glorious spectacle, far more fascinating than the impassive cliffs that form the setting. Thus throughout the world the name Yosemite has come to spell waterfalls, just as Yellowstone stands for geysers.

Among the waterfalls of the Yosemite region are some of the highest and most spectacular of the free-leaping type, which is relatively rare in nature. Most waterfalls are cascades, broken in their descent by ledges. Leaping falls of great height can exist only where sheer, unbroken cliffs of great height cross the paths of streams, and the combination is not often realized. The Yosemite, however, contains several examples, and that fact accounts in large part for the valley's extraordinary scenic splendor. Those who view the Yosemite when its falls are dry behold only the empty stage upon which the living waters play their dramatic act.

Because of the small volume of the mountain streams that form them, the waterfalls of the Yosemite region are relatively slender, resembling shimmering veils or ribbons fluttering from the cliffs. Even the falls of the Merced River, though heavier, are not of the broad cataract type, for in the Yosemite region, which is a scant twenty miles from the crest of the Sierra Nevada, the Merced is still no larger than what is ordinarily termed a creek.

The falls of the Yosemite region may be divided into two categories: those that descend from steps in canyon floors and those that pour from the lips of hanging side valleys. To the first category belong the two falls which the Merced River makes in the short stretch of the Merced Canyon linking the Little Yosemite with the main valley. The river there makes a descent of 2,000 feet in a distance of one and a half miles. Throughout the lower half of this stretch the river tumbles in foaming cascades and rapids, but in the upper half it drops from the steps of the giant stairway, producing Vernal Fall and Nevada Fall, which are half a mile apart and which, curiously, trend not parallel but at right angles to each other.

The steps that form Vernal Fall and Nevada Fall owe their prominence to the fact that each is composed of massive granite, which the glacier could only abrade, while the steep front, or "riser," is determined by a vertical master joint below which the glacier was able to quarry away successive rock sheets. Neither cliff has yet been notched by the falling waters.

Vernal Fall, at the lower step, has the form of a broad water curtain that falls 317 feet from a straight, vertical cliff. It is distinguished from all other falls in the Yosemite region by the partly translucent, soft green hue of undivided water that shines through the foam at its surface. Iridescent clouds of mist rise from the pool and the rocks at the foot of the cliff and eddy about in the canyon, keeping the vegetation fresh and green. It was the suggestion of spring that inspired Dr. Bunnell to name this fall the Vernal. Scarcely less appropriate, however, was the Indian name Yan' o-pah ("cloud of water").

Between Vernal Fall and Nevada Fall the Merced makes several minor falls and cascades. One of these, the Silver Apron, ends at Emerald Pool. In the Silver Apron the water rushes down a gentle incline of smooth granite and spreads into a broad, thin, sparkling sheet. One small obstruction juts from the rock floor, and there the swift waters leap up to form an arched fountain of spray 3 to 5 feet high—a "water wheel," as it is locally termed. Sheet cascades of the Silver Apron type are not uncommon in the High Sierra. They are associated with the smooth floors of massive granite that are characteristic features of its glaciated canyons. The water wheel in the Silver Apron is a diminutive example of the much larger fountains of this kind for which the Tuolumne River is famous.

Nevada Fall, at the upper step, is nearly twice as high as Vernal Fall— to be precise, it measures 594 feet—but it is far less regular in form. At the top the water shoots in wild turmoil from a narrow channel. As the rockets of spray strike the sloping lower part of the cliff, they are flattened and reunited in a broad, resplendent apron. The dazzling whiteness of the fall suggested the name Nevada, which in Spanish means "snowy." By the Indians it was called Yo-wiye ("twisted fall").

The waterfalls of the second category, being intimately associated with the cliffs of the valley walls, also reflect the influences of the rock structure. The high leaping falls are associated with cliff faces determined by vertical or steeply inclined master joints; the broken cascades are associated with the hackled surfaces of rock masses traversed by numerous fractures; and the gliding cascades and spreading "aprons" are associated with large bodies of massive granite the smooth surfaces of which are due in part to exfoliation, in part to glacial grinding.

Among the most perfect examples of a free-leaping waterfall is Bridalveil Fall. From the lip of a steeply sloping gulch, the waters leap with great velocity over a vertical wall 620 feet high—a wall of massive granite that was cut thousands of years ago by the Yosemite Glacier. Wholly untrammeled, when not agitated by the wind, the fall descends in a beautiful parabolic curve, but, facing the daily up-valley breeze as it does, it more often sways and flutters like a filmy fabric.

Unlike most of the Yosemite's great waterfalls, the Bridalveil hangs low in the landscape, the lip of the gulch from which it pours being only 850 feet above the valley floor. In spring and early summer, when the snow on the upland is melting fast, Bridalveil Fall swells to the proportions of a massive aerial torrent. Striking the rocks and pools at its base with tremendous impact, it sends out great clouds of spray, suffused by the afternoon sun with prismatic colors. Most sightseers, however, know the Bridalveil only as it presents itself in midsummer, in the filmy, veil-like form which suggests its name. The prismatic colors persist, but only in a simple rainbow arc. In autumn, when the volume is still smaller, the water, wholly divided into spray, is sometimes blown up and back into the gulch whence it came by a strong puff of the daily up-valley breeze. At night the fall is almost invariably accompanied by a downward rush of chilled air from the gulch above that violently sways the shrubs and trees about its base. It was probably because of this phenomenon that the Indians named the fall Po'ho-no, the "fall of the puffing winds."

In these characteristics as well as in its height and form the Bridalveil closely resembles the celebrated Staubbach in the Lauterbrunnen Valley of Switzerland. But its setting is far more remarkable, for it leaps from the end of the imposing promontory surmounted by the Cathedral Rocks, which juts more than a mile into Yosemite Valley.

Highest of all is Ribbon Fall, which descends 1,612 feet from an upland vale to the west of El Capitan. However, since it is confined in a narrow, sheer-walled recess and does not make a clear leap throughout, it can hardly be classed as a free-leaping fall. (The recess, incidentally, has not been worn by the slender torrent, but appears to have been elaborated mainly by the spray, which, freezing in the joints of the vertically sheeted granite, loosens thin plates and slabs and makes them available for removal by the rushing water.) Ribbon Creek, which drains an area of only a few square miles, often dries up in autumn, but in early summer it attains sufficient volume to give its fall great splendor. Clouds of spray then shoot out from the base of the recess and swirl from the opening at the top like steam from a geyser hole.

Another fall of the slender ribbon type is Silver Strand, really the cascade of Meadow Brook, which is situated in an angular recess between Old Inspiration Point and Stanford Point, near the lower end of the valley. It falls 1,170 feet, but seldom has volume enough to leap clear of the inclined cliff face. By midsummer it usually dries up. Its foot is about 2,000 feet above the bottom of the valley.

Of peculiar interest because its form is clearly determined by the structure of the cliffs is the long chain of falls of Sentinel Creek in the recess west of Sentinel Rock. The upper falls, which have a total drop of 1,500 feet, descend by successive rock steps of 50 to 200 feet. Below them the main Sentinel Fall makes a clear leap over a sheer wall 500 feet high.

Surpassing all the other falls in height and splendor are the Yosemite Falls. Though produced by a mere tributary of the Merced River, it seems fitting that they should bear the name of the valley, for, even more than El Capitan and Half Dome, they have given the Yosemite its wide renown.

The Yosemite Falls are composed of the great Upper Fall, the lesser Lower Fall, and an intermediate chain of cascades. These have a combined drop of 2,565 feet, or almost half a mile, and fall the entire distance from the upland to the bottom of the valley. Upper Yosemite Fall, which descends 1,430 feet, is easily the valley's chief ornament and, in early summer, when the upland streams are at high stage from melting snow, attains a magnificence unequaled by any other fall on this continent. It is, so far as can be ascertained at the time of writing, the highest free-leaping waterfall in existence. Lower Yosemite Fall, with a drop of only 320 feet,

seems insignificant by comparison. Yet it is twice as high as Niagara, and
at its best affords an impressive spectacle.

Viewed from afar, Upper Yosemite Fall seems to drop vertically from
the lip of the hanging valley, but in reality, like Bridalveil Fall, it makes
a free, parabolic leap of 1,360 feet, the upper 70 feet of the fall descending through a chute worn in the face of the cliff. Below the chute the fall
leaps clear of the cliff, although the latter is inclined at an angle of 80°,
and, describing a curve through space, clears even the bulging lower
part of the cliff, which projects more than 100 feet beyond the top. Perhaps a truer conception of the height of the fall will be gained from the
statement that it is about nine times as high as Niagara Falls. The Eiffel
Tower in Paris measures 987 feet—little more than two-thirds the height
of Upper Yosemite Fall.

Because of the resistance offered by the air, the water deploys gradually
into a broad curtain of lacelike spray. The more concentrated parts shoot
down in arrowy masses resembling comets. The tremendous force of the
fall is evident from the deafening reports. It seems incredible that a
transparent fabric of mere spray, which at times is flung to one side or is
even lifted bodily by eddying breezes, should impinge so heavily. Muir
once undertook to pass between fall and cliff on the narrow ledge that
extends part way across the cliff front about 450 feet above the base—Fern
Ledge, he called it—but a mass of spray swayed against the cliff, and he
barely succeeded in groping out alive.

The cliff over which Upper Yosemite Fall leaps was produced by the
splitting off of a huge sheet of rock along a master joint. A part of the
sheet still clings to the cliff to the east of the fall. It forms the amazing
tapering rock monument, 1,500 feet high, known as the Lost Arrow.

On the cliff face the spray freezes in winter, but it usually drops off
without doing much damage for lack of fractures into which it might
penetrate. But the slabs of frozen spray that fall from the cliff when loosened by the heat of the sun accumulate to form a great white cone that
sometimes reaches a height of 200 or 300 feet. And behind this cone the
freezing spray and water have chiseled out along a horizontal master joint
a cavern that extends 40 feet into the cliff. That cavern and the Lost
Arrow, the writer holds, are the two most astounding pieces of rock sculpture in the valley.

At the foot of Upper Yosemite Fall the waters converge toward a half-
bowl of polished granite; thence the stream, remade, dashes through a
narrow, winding gorge. After a boisterous descent of 815 feet it reaches
the edge of a recess in the lowermost tier of cliffs and leaps to the floor
of the valley, producing Lower Yosemite Fall. This fall also makes a
clear leap at times of high water.

Another leaping fall is the Illilouette, which descends 370 feet from the mouth of the hanging valley of Illilouette Creek. Ensconced in a deep gorge, it is visible from only a few points and is relatively little known, yet in volume it is the largest fall made by any of the Merced's tributaries. In early summer it presents a fascinating spectacle, viewed from the Glacier Point Trail, as the water disappears thundering into a dark abyss of seemingly measureless depth.

Two of the minor falls have each a distinctive character. The Staircase Falls, back of Camp Curry, tumble, as the name implies, from successive stairlike rock steps, 1,300 feet in all. Royal Arches Cascade glides rather than drops 1,250 feet from the steeply inclined, smooth cliff west of the Royal Arches. This continuous ribbon of foaming water is the only representative in Yosemite Valley of a special type of cascade associated with smooth walls of massive granite, of which there are many in the upper Yosemite region and adjoining parts of the High Sierra.

The Merced Gorge below the Yosemite Valley also abounds in waterfalls. There is one at the mouth of each hanging side valley. The largest are the Cascades, at the elbow bend of the gorge, which are formed by the joint waters of Cascade Creek and Tamarack Creek. Unlike most of the major falls of the Yosemite region, they are cascades in the real sense, irregularly broken in their total descent of about 500 feet.

The Little Yosemite receives no tributary streams of notable volume and consequently is graced by no large waterfalls; but it does have numerous ribbon cascades similar to the Royal Arches Cascade. Most of these flow only a short time in early summer, being fed by the snow on the forested uplands. They resemble parallel ribbons of silver filigree. Those on Cascade Cliffs fall fully 1,500 feet. As they dry up they leave dark bands or stripes on the cliffs resembling the stains that disfigure city buildings. Their inky hue is produced by minute purplish-black lichens that maintain life on the sun-heated cliffs in spite of prolonged desiccation. Longest and most spectacular are the ribbon cascades that glide down the stupendous cliff face of Clouds Rest, on the south side of Tenaya Canyon. They are fed by patches of snow that linger in the shaded recesses until midsummer. They make descents of 2,000 to 3,000 feet.

In Tenaya Canyon, a mile above Mirror Lake, are the falls and cascades by which Snow Creek drops from its hanging valley on the north side of the canyon. They have a total fall of about 2,000 feet, but, being deeply situated in a gorge of their own cutting, they cannot be viewed in their entirety from any one point and are little known to the public. Another waterfall that deserves to be better known is Tenaya Cascade, at the head of Tenaya Canyon. It glides down a steeply inclined, marvelously smooth 600-foot cliff of undivided granite. It is strictly a ribbon cascade, but is the most voluminous and impressive of its kind. Indeed, it is to be counted among the major waterfalls of the Yosemite region.

None of the waterfalls in the great canyons farther south in the Sierra Nevada can compare with those of the Yosemite in height and striking individuality. Rainbow Fall, on the Middle Fork of the San Joaquin, to the south of the Devils Postpile, makes a single leap of 150 feet over a cliff of columnar basalt, part of a volcanic flow that came from the direction of the Devils Postpile. Of interest also are the Volcano Falls, by which Golden Trout Creek descends from its upland valley into the Kern Canyon, but these falls are cascades rather than leaping falls.

Whether Yosemite Valley possesses the highest waterfall in the world is a question that cannot yet be answered with absolute certainty, for even today the more remote mountain regions of the earth have not been completely explored. The following list includes all the high falls on which definite information is available. Mile-wide cataracts produced by rivers of large volume, such as the Niagara, Victoria, or Iguazu, are omitted as being in a separate class. Only free-leaping falls are listed.

Tueeulala Fall, in Hetch Hetchy Valley, is, at its best, comparable to Upper Yosemite Fall, but its total drop is estimated at 1,000 feet and it makes a clear leap of only 600 feet. The Multnomah Falls, in the gorge of the Columbia River, in Oregon, make an essentially unbroken descent of about 700 feet. Snoqualmie Fall, in the state of Washington, is comparable to Vernal Fall but about 49 feet lower. Lower Yellowstone Fall measures 308 feet, or 9 feet less than the Vernal.

Of the numerous waterfalls in British Columbia the Takakkaw Falls, in the Yoho Valley, are the best known. They make a total descent of 1,346 feet, including a partly free leap of about 900 feet. In the upper Yoho Valley are also the Twin Falls, said to measure about 600 feet. Less well known is the great leaping fall in the upper Bella Coola Valley, which, so far as can be ascertained, drops 800, possibly 1,000 feet.

The deep fiords of the Alaska coast are rich in falling waters, but most of these are cascades. Muir believed that he saw in a bay of the Endicott Arm of Stephens Pass, which he referred to as Yosemite Bay, leaping falls of greater height than those of Yosemite Valley. The topographic maps of the locality, however, give no hint of the presence of cliffs "five or six thousand feet high," and it seems probable that Muir overestimated the height of the waterfalls as well as of the cliffs.

The many waterfalls in the Hawaiian Islands consist mostly of broken cascades. However, the Akaka Falls, above Honomu, on the island of Hawaii, make a free leap of about 400 feet; and the Hiilawe Falls, visible from Waipio Bay, leap fully 500 feet.

Basaseachic Fall, in the Sierra Tarahumara of Chihuahua, Mexico, makes a clear leap variously estimated at 827 to 1,040 feet. In the brief spring season this fall rivals the Upper Yosemite in scenic splendor.

Tequendama Fall, on the Bogotá River, Colombia, bears a resemblance to Nevada Fall. It exceeds that fall in volume but measures about 150 feet less. Kaieteur Fall, on the Potaro River, British Guiana, a water curtain of the Vernal type, descends about 740 feet. It is one of the highest falls produced by a river of considerable volume.

Among the many waterfalls that adorn the steep-walled fiords of Norway are the celebrated Vöring Fos, which makes an almost unbroken descent of 850 feet; the Valur Fos, with a more irregularly shaped fall of 1,150 feet; the Vettis Fos, with an almost clear leap of 853 feet.

The most widely known fall of the slender Yosemite type has already been mentioned, the Staubbach, in Switzerland. It descends about 600 feet, and is comparable to the Bridalveil in volume.

The falls of Gavarnie, in an alpine amphitheater of rare beauty on the French side of the Pyrenees, are noted as the highest waterfalls in Europe—1,385 feet, 55 feet less than Upper Yosemite Fall—but they consist mostly of broken, interlacing cascades.

The Kalambo River, which forms the boundary between Northern Rhodesia and Tanganyika Territory, makes two falls, the upper of which is, so far as can be ascertained, not less than 1,200 feet. The volume is probably greater than that of the Merced River.

The Sharavati River, in southern India, descends from the Deccan Plateau by the Gersoppa Falls, which are estimated to be about 830 feet high. Of these the Raja makes an essentially clear leap.

Wooloomumbi Fall, on a branch of the Macleay River, in New South Wales, Australia, measures about 900 feet. It not only leaps clear but shoots far out from the cliff, owing to its momentum.

Into the waters of Milford Sound, New Zealand, plunge the Stirling and Bowen falls. The Stirling makes a fairly regular leap of 504 feet; the Bowen descends 550 feet in the form of a parted curtain. Both have a volume comparable to that of the Illilouette. Highest of the New Zealand falls and among the highest in the world are the Sutherland Falls, which drop into the canyon of the Arthur River from a typical hanging valley. They consist of a chain of three falls having a total descent of 1,904 feet. Their respective measurements are, beginning with the uppermost, 815, 751, and 338 feet. Only the lowermost makes a clear leap.

From this review it will be seen that Upper Yosemite Fall leads all the other leaping falls thus far known in height. The fact gains in significance when it is considered that it is but one of a chain of falls having a total descent of 2,565 feet. Few regions besides the Yosemite possess sheer declivities of that magnitude.

9 The little ice age of historic times

There is a widely prevalent impression that the Sierra glaciers of our own times are relics left from the Ice Age. But recent studies leave little doubt that all remnants of the vast ice mantle which covered the higher parts of the Sierra Nevada during the Ice Age melted away thousands of years ago, and that the present small glaciers represent a new generation born only about 4,000 years ago—thousands of years after the Ice Age came to an end.

The Sierra Nevada now bears about sixty small glaciers on its long-drawn crest. Southernmost of the series are the two glacierets that lie side by side on the northern flanks of Middle Palisade and the crest that leads eastward from that peak to the Thumb. They are situated in latitude 37° 04′ N. Vestigial remnants of glacier ice occur in shady cirques as far south as the vicinity of Whitney Pass, latitude 36° 33′ N., but these small remnants of stagnant ice can hardly be counted as some of the Sierra's living glaciers.

Most of the Sierra glaciers are of the cirque type and lie deeply ensconced in north- or northeast-facing amphitheaters with high walls. Some of the smaller ones cling to the northern or northeastern bases of bold comb ridges and peaks. All occupy sites in which snow blown by the prevailing westerly and southwesterly winds is trapped in large quantities and where its wastage is minimized not only by the prolonged shade of the cliffs, but also, during the brief hours when the sun shines into the hollows, by the large angle of incidence with which its rays impinge upon the sloping surface of the ice. Toward the end of summer, in average years, the glaciers and glacierets are the only white patches that remain in the landscape of the High Sierra. In places sheltered from both winds and sun, snowdrifts occasionally survive from one winter to the next, but they are not perennial.

It is not to be supposed, however, that the glaciers of the Sierra Nevada lie in the zone of maximum snow precipitation. On the western slope of the range, that zone reaches from altitudes of 4,000 to 5,000 feet on up to altitudes of 8,000 to 9,000 feet, but the glaciers are situated either on the main crest or on subsidiary crests, at altitudes ranging from about 11,000 feet at the northern boundary of Yosemite National Park (latitude 38° 06' N.) to 12,500 feet at Middle Palisade (latitude 37° 04' N.).

For the extreme crest of the Sierra Nevada, accurate data on snowfall are not available and, indeed, would be almost impossible to obtain, for there the winds are more potent than gravity as distributors of snow. They lift the storm clouds and the snowflakes that condense from them over the top of the range, and they pick up much of the snow that has fallen on the ground and drive it upslope, releasing it only as they eddy in the lee of ridges and cliffs. Westward-slanting summit platforms such as those of Mount Whitney and Mount Langley never bear more than a thin coating of snow. Often they are blown partly bare, the powdery snow extending eastward in shimmering banners, to be diffused and in part lost over the warmer slopes below. Only rough estimates of snowfall can be made for the crestal portions of the Sierra Nevada, the snow conservatories of the range, but there is good reason to believe that it is considerably less than the prodigious amounts measured at lower levels.

The largest and best known of the Sierra glaciers are the East Lyell and the West Lyell glaciers on Mount Lyell, and the neighboring Maclure Glacier, all in Yosemite National Park, and the Palisade Glacier, farther south, at the head of Big Pine Creek on the east side of the divide. Each glacier measures a scant mile in length, from the distinctive crevasse at its head, the *bergschrund*, to the terminus. The majority of Sierra

glaciers average about half a mile in length, and some of the glacierets
are scarcely a quarter of a mile long. Because of their small size they
were mistaken for mere snow fields by the members of the Geological
Survey of California, who first beheld them in the early 'sixties. It was
John Muir who in 1871 first identified some of the alleged snow fields
as small but true glaciers. In 1872 he proved his case by careful measurements on the Maclure Glacier, by means of stakes planted in its surface,
which demonstrated that the ice moves at the rate of about one inch a day.

That the Sierra glaciers, down to the smallest glacieret, are all living
glaciers and not snow fields is evident from the following observed facts:
(1) The white snow at the surface grades downward into granular névé
and finally into gray, laminated ice. (2) The ice mass is gravitating slowly
downward with true glacier motion, as is unmistakably indicated by
the *bergschrund* at its head and, at lower levels, of other crevasses that
rend its body where the glacier moves over obstructions or descends from
ledges or steps in the rock bed. (3) Each of these ice bodies is encircled
at its lower end by ridge-shaped accumulations of rock debris which, it is
evident from their composition, are true glacial moraines.

Viewed in late summer, when the landscape of the Sierra Nevada is
almost wholly divested of snow, these small, scattered, more or less isolated patches of ice give the impression of being the last lingering remnants of the extensive glaciers and ice fields that covered the higher parts
of the range during the Ice Age. So it has been assumed that these small
glaciers, like the ice caps on Greenland, Iceland, and Antarctica, are
dwindling relics inherited from glacial times. But that belief is based
upon an implicit assumption that ever since the end of the Ice Age climatic conditions have improved rather steadily up to the present time.
The fact that glaciers throughout the world are now gradually shrinking
in size and have been shrinking for several decades would seem to lend
support to that belief. Yet there is at hand today a large body of evidence indicating beyond possible doubt that climatic conditions, far
from ameliorating steadily throughout postglacial time, have fluctuated
strongly and, from the human point of view, with almost incredible ups
and downs.

Taking the duration of the postglacial interval as a round 9,000 years
(an approximation from the count of Swedish scientists), it seems that
already during the first 2,000 years after the end of the Ice Age temperatures rose above the present level. As they continued to rise, there
ensued, in the middle part of the postglacial interval, a period of great
warmth, such as civilized man has not experienced, lasting about 3,000
years. It is commonly referred to in the literature as the postglacial climatic optimum. Then temperatures declined gradually, and during the

last millennium B.C. they dropped rather abruptly to the present level.

Since then, throughout the Christian Era, there has been a succession of short but sharp fluctuations. The Middle Ages were, for the most part, a period of moderate, genial warmth. The Norsemen who colonized Iceland and Greenland toward the end of the tenth century were favored by relatively mild conditions, and met no ice floes or icebergs on their voyages to the eastern coast of Greenland. On the shores of Greenland they found thriving forests where now the barren ground is permanently frozen; this is proved by the fact that their graves, now encased in frozen soil, are pierced by the roots of trees that have long since ceased to grow in Greenland. It is equally clear that favorable conditions did not last beyond the twelfth century.

During the next 400 years the climate became increasingly variable and inclement. In the Alps at least fourteen major and minor glacial advances seem to have occurred between 1595 and 1939. Climatic severity reached a peak toward the end of the sixteenth century and in the first half of the seventeenth, in northern Europe and the Alps of Switzerland, Savoy, Italy, and the Tyrol. Villages that had been in existence for hundreds of years were overwhelmed by rapidly advancing glaciers—glaciers that until then had been so small and so far up among the peaks that no one had ever thought they might become a menace. Other Alpine settlements and much valuable pastureland were devastated by recurrent floods of meltwater, and high mountain passes that from time immemorial had been used as summer trade routes became blocked by ice.

The present glaciers of the Alps, in spite of recent recession, still bury many works constructed by man in the Middle Ages. In the valley of Chamonix the silver mine after which the village of Argentière was named is still beneath ice; so likewise, in the Veni Valley, is the village of St. Jean de Perthuis, which was overwhelmed by the ice about the year 1600.

These first catastrophic glacier advances were followed by others of nearly the same magnitude, especially in the eighteenth century. The worst took place in 1719, 1743, and from 1770 to 1779. In 1719 the glaciers advanced so rapidly that the terrified villagers appealed to the authorities to take measures to drive the glaciers back. Whereupon, it is related, they did go back—but not permanently. In the intervals between advances the glaciers receded or stagnated, but the mountain passes remained blocked, and no one dared to rebuild the destroyed villages on their original sites.

The first half of the nineteenth century was much like the preceding 200 years. When Agassiz wrote his classic *Étude sur les glaciers,* in 1840, the sharp glacier advance of 1818–1820 was still fresh in the memories of men. Perhaps, viewed in retrospect, Agassiz's departure for the United States in 1846 was a misfortune for glacial science, for the last major glacial advance and the second greatest of historic times reached its climax in 1850, and it cannot be doubted that Agassiz would have been the richer for having watched it run its course.

The year 1850 appears to have been the turning point in the modern glacial history of central Europe; for since then the trend of climate not only in Europe but throughout the world has been distinctly milder, and glaciers have been in recession almost everywhere. That temperatures have risen during the past century is clearly revealed by graphs from meteorologic stations in various parts of the world; but to anyone acquainted with the records of glacier oscillations in the same period it must be evident that the glaciers supply a far more precise and detailed record.[1] The European glacier records, based on systematic annual measurements since 1874, show that around 1890 the recession was interrupted by a moderate readvance, and by lesser readvances or halts in the periods 1910–1913, 1917–1920, and 1926. Plotted on a graph, the recurring readvances look like small peaks on a curve descending with ever-increasing pitch. The present continuation of glacial recession which is threatening the existence of our western glaciers is an accelerated phase of the process of deglaciation. Clearly it has no connection with the end of the Great Ice Age; it follows upon what may be termed the "little ice age" of the historic period.

There is good reason to believe that the present glaciers in the Sierra Nevada are products of this "little ice age" and represent a new generation of ice bodies born not many centuries ago. The moraines that encircle their fronts are very fresh in appearance in comparison with the youngest recessional moraines of the Ice Age that lie below them in the canyons. Embankments commonly rise 20 to 50 feet above the adjacent ice and enclose the ends of the glaciers like massive crescentic walls. In reality, they are made up of many small terminal moraines, laid against and on top of each other, as is clearly shown in instances where individual moraines lie spread out in a series, one behind another, with concentrically curving crests. They record for each glacier many repeated readvances, all of approximately the same magnitude.

---

[1] Glaciers are extremely sensitive to climatic fluctuations and register them more vividly than do streams, springs, lakes, or vegetation. Since man has so delicately, so daringly adjusted some of his great agricultural and engineering enterprises and their dependent industries to existing climatic conditions, it behooves him, for the good of his complex civilization, to keep a close watch on climatic changes or fluctuations, however slight and transient. Hence the present international interest in the observation and measurement of glaciers. In the United States the Committee on Glaciers of the American Geophysical Union is the central agency charged with the responsibility for systematic measurement and recording of current variations in volume of American glaciers, the interpretation of such variations, and related research in all parts of the country, including Alaska.

How many centuries of glacier oscillations are represented by these morainal accumulations it is difficult to estimate, but the youthful appearance of even the outermost ridges suggests strongly that they do not date from the Ice Age. The blocks and slabs on them are still loosely piled together, and the slopes have not yet everywhere assumed the angle of rest for such materials. In scrambling over these ridges even an experienced mountaineer must exercise great caution lest he dislodge not merely small fragments but boulders weighing many tons, which are ready to slide or roll down at a touch.

The recent origin of these moraines is attested, further, by the fact that some of them still have a core of "dead," or "stagnant" glacier ice; they are really remnants of the former terminal portions of the glaciers themselves, preserved under a thick insulating cover of morainal debris. As this buried ice is melted locally by water percolating from the glaciers, cave-ins may destroy the continuity of the moraine crests. Even the unusually massive embankment that encloses the Palisade Glacier (the largest glacier in the southern part of the range) seems to be subject to such cave-ins, and to them probably owes the central sag in its crest.

Having spent many a summer tramping over and mapping the long ridgelike moraines which the glaciers of the Ice Age left on the western slope of the Sierra Nevada, and training his eyes to detect the slight variations that distinguish moraines of different ages, the writer was struck by the evidences of extreme youth in the "raw" moraines enclosing the glacier fronts. With due allowance for the fact that they are situated at high altitudes, above the zone of vegetation, and therefore are destined to remain barren, whereas the moraines of the Ice Age in the canyons below bear considerable vegetation, it seems probable that the two sets of moraines may differ in age by several thousand years. Also, significantly, the younger moraines are apparently not connected with the older moraines by any graded series of intermediate age.

May it not be possible, then, that these fresh-looking moraines are not simply the youngest of the recessional moraines left by the retreating glaciers of the Ice Age, but the products of new ice bodies that were formed relatively recently in the cirques left vacant by the vanished glaciers of the Ice Age?

The present recession of small glaciers shows that they cannot hold their own under current climatic conditions. From the annual measurements of glaciers in and near Yosemite National Park, it is evident that they are delicately adjusted to climatic conditions and respond sensitively to any departure from the norm, either in precipitation or temperature. Even a single winter of scanty snowfall followed by an unusually warm summer reduces them at an alarming rate. They appear to be losing 3 to 6 feet annually from their surfaces, which is a rapid rate in view of the fact that they are only 200 to 300 feet thick. It is obvious that a sustained decrease in snowfall, accompanied by slightly higher temperatures, would destroy them all in less than a century. Indeed, several have vanished within the last half-century, including the little glacier under Merced Peak which John Muir discovered, to his surprise and joy, in 1871. Throughout the High Sierra are scores if not hundreds of empty cirques, the fresh, unweathered moraines of which leave little doubt that they contained small glaciers of this type during the nineteenth century.

It is not likely, then, that the existing Sierra glaciers could have survived the excessive heat of the climatic optimum for 3,000 years. The warmth of that remarkable period is difficult to estimate in thermometric degrees, but some conception can be obtained from the character of the plant and animal remains that have been found entombed in postglacial peat bogs. Warmth-loving vegetation such as now prevails in the Carolinas and Virginia then flourished as far north as New England and southern Canada, and extinct subtropical animals (e.g., the ground sloth, President Jefferson's famed *Megalonyx*) roamed as far north as the Great Lakes and Minnesota.

Most important in its bearing on the history of the glaciers, however, is the discovery that in the Alps as well as in the mountains of Scandinavia the timber line on the mountains formerly lay more than a thousand feet above its present level. For this implies that the snow line also lay more than a thousand feet higher, and that must have spelled the death of thousands of small glaciers lying at relatively low altitudes. Only glaciers originating at altitudes several thousand feet above the present snow line could survive.

In North America data of this sort are very scarce, mainly because not enough search for them has been made, but in a few localities, notably on Mount Hood, Oregon, and on the Fairweather Range of southern Alaska, evidence has been found that vegetation belonging in fairly low, warm zones formerly flourished at altitudes near or above the present timber line—and that could have happened only during a long period of unusual warmth such as the climatic optimum.

A thousand-foot upward shift of the snow line would not have stripped the ice from all our western mountains. Mount Rainier, the ice-laden summit of which now rises fully 5,000 feet above the snow line, never lost all its glaciers, but the Sierra Nevada surely did, for it has at present no snow line. Even its highest peaks with broad summits bear no perpetual ice. The theoretical snow line lies well above them, probably not less than 2,000 feet above the small glaciers. The latter are able to exist because of the exceptionally favorable conditions which their cirques afford for the entrapment of wind-blown snow in winter and its conservation in summer. Each cirque has a microclimate of its own that renders it just possible for a small ice mass to persist under present conditions. When the snow line rose another thousand feet higher, the timberline zone rose to the cirques, and in the warmth of that zone the last glacierets perished. There is, then, good reason to believe that the present glaciers of the Sierra Nevada are new, or "modern," glaciers that came into existence during the "little ice age."

How old are the glaciers of our times likely to be? The answer cannot be found in the glaciers themselves, but fortunately a clue to their probable age is supplied by the life history of Owens Lake in the Owens Valley, which has justly earned the name of "the land of little rain." That lake, situated at the eastern base of the Sierra Nevada, was fed— before man interfered with natural conditions by appropriating for his own purposes the water of its tributary, the Owens River—almost wholly by meltwater from the snow fields and glaciers on the range, and during glacial and postglacial times must have been affected by the same climatic variations as the glaciers. Like all other salt lakes occupying basins from which there is no overflow, Owens Lake has become briny because, as its waters evaporate into the parched desert air, the mineral salts dissolved in them are left behind and become progressively more concentrated.

This circumstance affords a basis for the calculation of the age of the lake. From the amount of salt which Owens Lake contained in 1912, before the diversion of water from the Owens River to the Los Angeles Aqueduct, and from the known quantities of salt which the river then brought each year into the lake, it has been computed that all the salt present in Owens Lake could readily have accumulated in less than 4,000 years. Obviously, the present Owens Lake could not have been in existence continuously since the last glacial climax of the Ice Age. It must be a new lake of relatively recent origin.

The 4,000 years indicated for the age of the lake just about covers the duration of the cool period that followed the climatic optimum. It therefore seems an inescapable conclusion that the large Owens Lake of the Ice Age dried up during that warm period because of deficiency of snow and ice in the Sierra Nevada and higher temperatures that promoted more rapid evaporation; and that the present Owens Lake is a new-born pool, formed, when cooler and snowier conditions returned, within a "freshened" basin in which the accumulation of salt began anew. Both the modern Owens Lake (now virtually dry as the result of artificial diversion) and the modern glaciers on the Sierra Nevada appear to be products of the "little ice age," and are of about the same age.

It is quite possible that 4,000 years is a maximum figure, for, although the salt crust left from the ancient glacial lake must have become buried during the warm period under layers of gravel, sand, and silt which the mountain streams brought down, some of the salt may have become incorporated in the modern lake; if so, the calculation is based on too large a quantity. But it is interesting to reflect that even if the present Sierra glaciers were 4,000 years old they would still be 500 years younger than that greatest structure of antiquity, the Pyramid of Cheops, which, according to recent researches, was built between 2656 and 2633 B.C.

Thus it becomes necessary to readjust our thinking to a concept which places the Sierra Nevada in a wholly new light: that for a stretch of several thousand years the range probably bore no glaciers, and that the small glaciers of our own times "came back" as recently as about 2,000 B.C.

What has happened in the Sierra Nevada has doubtless happened on many other western mountain ranges where the glaciers were affected by the same postglacial fluctuations of climate. This is evident from their analogous systems of moraines. Other ranges contain the same fresh-looking moraines, many with glacier-ice cores, arranged in compact concentric series or combined in one or two massive compound embankments. Not only the Sierra glaciers but hundreds of ice bodies of the cirque type on the Cascade Range, the Rocky Mountains, and the great ranges of western Canada and Alaska are evidently of recent origin.

Sufficient data are not at hand to permit definite discrimination between reborn glaciers and glaciers which have survived from the Ice Age, but enough is known to warrant the statement that probably most of the glaciers in the Rocky Mountains south of the Canadian boundary and all the small cirque glaciers on the Cascade Range and the Olympic Mountains are reborn, or "modern," glaciers. Only the major ice streams on Mount Rainier, Mount Baker, Mount Olympus, Glacier Peak, and perhaps a few other lofty peaks in the Pacific Northwest are likely to have persisted since the Ice Age.

As for the huge trunk glaciers of British Columbia and Alaska, which measure as much as thirty and forty miles in length, it can hardly be doubted that they have existed uninterruptedly throughout postglacial time. But in view of their large oscillations in response to the feeble climatic variations of the past 100 years, it is evident, also, that they suffered tremendous reductions in volume and extent during the warm, dry period that preceded the last 4,000 years. Vast mountain areas in British Columbia and Alaska that are now heavily and continuously mantled with snow and ice must then have been in large part bare. The glaciers there must since have been regenerated on a grand scale compared with those in the continental United States. It may truly be said that we are now living in an epoch of renewed but moderate glaciation—a "little ice age."

It does not necessarily follow, however, that we are at the beginning of another great ice age, nor even of a substage of the glaciation which seemingly continues in Greenland and in Antarctica. Neither is it to be supposed that the sundry fluctuations and general recession of the glaciers in the last few decades necessarily herald the end of our "little ice age." It is much more likely that they represent one of the mild fluctuations that have occurred repeatedly in the last 4,000 years. The glaciers will recede for a time and then will again advance, as they have done many times in the past, if we may judge from the multiple character of "modern" moraines.

In these multiple moraines are recorded, though rather obscurely, the vicissitudes of the glaciers of the "little ice age." They constitute a record linking this new chapter of glacier history with the present, and their interpretation is of considerable interest to students of hydrology, climatology, ecology, and archaeology. But that record is still to be read.